Fundamentals of **LAYOUT**

**FOR NEWSPAPER AND
MAGAZINE ADVERTISING,
FOR PAGE DESIGN OF
PUBLICATIONS AND
FOR BROCHURES**

F. H. WILLS

**DOVER PUBLICATIONS, INC.
NEW YORK**

Published in Canada by General Publishing Company, Ltd., 30 Lesmill Road, Don Mills, Toronto, Ontario.
Published in the United Kingdom by Constable and Company, Ltd., 10 Orange Street, London WC 2.

This Dover edition, first published in 1971, is an unabridged and unaltered republication of the work originally published in 1965 under the title *Complete Introduction to Fundamentals of Layout*. The work is reprinted by special arrangement with Sterling Publishing Company, Inc., 419 Park Avenue South, New York City 10016, publisher of the original edition.

International Standard Book Number: 0-486-21279-3
Library of Congress Catalog Card Number: 78-166431

Manufactured in the United States of America
Dover Publications, Inc.
180 Varick Street
New York, N. Y. 10014

ACKNOWLEDGMENTS

The author and the publishers wish to express their thanks to the typefounders, publishers, printers, advertising consultants and graphic artists for their kind provision of typefaces, illustrated material and tables.

Translated by Kenneth T. Dutfield

Contents

PREFACE

ADVERTISING as a special profession is still comparatively young. On the other hand, the demand for qualified men and women is steadily increasing. Advertising is a complicated job for specialists, a many-sided and exacting task for the head and the hands. It is a science that has to be learned.

This handbook provides a clear survey of a decisive phase in the complicated process of creating advertisements: layout. It is based on the author's experience in advertising.

Layout, in its widest sense, means the realization of an advertising idea, the harmonious and vitally effective synthesis of three components: text, illustrations and white or colored space. These constitute the visible form in which advertising news has to reach the reader. Many illustrated examples of advertising creation from different parts of the world appear in this book, together with instructive drawings, to form an aesthetic standard on which special, topical requirements can be built up.

THE EYE is the most important intermediary in people's contact with their environment. All the other senses are secondary to vision, but the intensity of the reaction produced in these other senses is the only yardstick by which we judge the effect of what is seen.

The earliest form of communication was the spoken word. It necessarily involved the presence of a partner. Later, man discovered how to make himself understood by means of pictures, how to fix and give substantial form, beyond the limits of speech, to information, desires and ideas. Only afterwards did the written language come into being, evolving from pictograms. So pictures and writing sprang from a single source.

These two forms of expression have diverged more and more widely and become increasingly diversified in the course of years. Their frontiers still overlap, however, although we are generally accustomed to thinking of them as thoroughly separate spheres. Are traffic signs or astronomical and meteorological symbols pictures? Isn't it truer to say that we *read* them? Does the mind translate the circle used as a symbol for the sun, the crescent for the moon, the "dangerous corner" sign at the roadside, and the red and green of the traffic lights, into words and sentences? Every picture gives its message to us in the same way the written or printed word does: pictures are even read from left to right. There may be many pictures we do not understand; they tell us nothing because they are "written in a foreign language."

In a host of different ways mankind throughout the ages has used both means of communicating ideas, but only the present age has made the picture supreme as a method of conveying instruction and information. We cannot envisage life without pictures, any more than we can imagine human existence today without printing. The triumph of the picture was assured by its universal acceptance: it is more versatile and "readable," less easily misunderstood than the written word. Moreover, there are no "pictorial illiterates."

Basic Principles of Layout

Innumerable books exist about writing and about illustration in all languages, but little has been written about the combination of script and pictures, especially as it is realized in advertising, books, magazines and other printed matter. This book therefore will attempt to deal with principles and essential techniques for adapting pictures and writing to each other.

Many people are at work, daily and hourly, in making advertising influential, in designing magazines and illustrated books. Because of the lack of literature on the subject, recruits to the profession usually have to begin at the beginning. The same mistakes are made again and again, while students become adept in their art. Knowledge reveals itself to them only after arduous study. But there were many students and masters before them who arrived at the same conclusions and who simply neglected to write them down for the sake of their posterity.

The duty of layout—the theme of this book— is to give visual form to all graphic expression that has the purpose of advertising. Typography and illustration, as far as their size and character are concerned, are determined by layout. The layout arranges these elements, if they are ready to be formalized, and adapts them to each other. It sketches new ideas and with them forms the basis for interplay of text and illustrations. Layout determines the most suitable form for an advertising project —be it a newspaper advertisement, brochure, catalogue or picture page. It is the foundation on which the creative artist and the technician build. Every created form gains effectiveness from a combination of tensions, harmonies and contrasts.

Although the idea of layout is often variously interpreted, so that its limits sometimes comprise anything from rough sketches to finished drawings, the term as used here stands for a composition, a design, a ground-plan of the elements in a piece of work to be printed. The graphic artist works out the details, but the layout is the foundation of the team operation which produces the finished "eye-catcher."

This handbook is not just a collection of patterns or recipes. It sets out the essential conditions, gives warning of possible mistakes and points the way to success. It is based on experience which has never been allowed to crystallize into a fixed routine of work. It evaluates what is good—from whatever source the good may come—from the point of view of its usefulness. It is broad-minded enough to welcome the unique, exotic newcomers that resist every attempt to remodel them.

THE LAYOUT TEAM

It is only possible for those engaged in creative work to scale the heights—whether it be an intellectual, scientific, technical pursuit or one involving craftsmanship—if the practical foundations of the work are fully understood. There are no great painters who cannot draw, no good architects ignorant of building methods, no fine photographers not well versed in the way light behaves and in the science of optics.

This book aims not only to make a functional and attractive unity of pictures and writing, but it intends to weld these two into a technically pure, intelligent and tasteful whole.

So, right at the start, this book is going to make demands on the reader, demands concerned with practical work rather than with theory. When you are well grounded in the foundations of technical knowledge in the field of words and pictures, as a graphic artist,

as a typographer or compositor, as an advertising copy specialist, photographer or art editor, you will reach your goal more rapidly.

This handbook is no substitute for apprenticeship. Nor, because of the particular way it deals with problems, can it take the place of specialized books on composition, printing, paper, reproduction processes and the economics of advertising. It communicates information needed for the creation of layouts, and gives instruction in the possibilities of composing text and pictures harmoniously or contrastingly. Then it requires you to put this knowledge to work.

The written word will be dealt with first and in detail. The same treatment will then be given to illustration in its main forms of manifestation: the photograph, the drawing and the painting.

Advertising through visual media—the most important of all forms of expression intended to influence people—demands a detailed knowledge of the ways in which an illustration can be used. Although the creative layout student may have to temper his tastes to the requirements of the commercial budget, he will eventually develop his own ideas on the balance to be struck between typography and illustration.

Specialization in advertising work now often means that the original planner of an advertisement, usually the commercial artist, no longer has any possibility of bringing his influence alone to bear on the final shaping of the work. Advertising agencies allocate an assignment to teams in such a way that only the combined efforts of the account executive or contact man, the copywriter, the artist, the layout man, the typographer and the compositor produce the finished work. The result is often an unsatisfactory compromise, despite the fact that everyone involved sincerely tries to do his best. Also, many a layout loses much of its effect by bad placement. Today more than ever, the layout man should not regard his work as finished when it leaves his hands, but should try to direct its further destiny. He in particular should be capable of shaping picture and copy into a unity which cannot be improved by any revision. This implies, apart from the obvious prerequisites of a strong sense of form and a wealth of ideas, detailed knowledge of technique.

Photographers too are one-sidedly trained if they have not attended a modern technical school. The advertisement photographer usually regards his work as finished when he hands it in after having thoroughly polished it up. A press photographer need not do even that. He has learned from experience that all the art editor wants from him is a glossy enlargement of the finished negative. The photographer seldom knows beforehand what his pictures will look like in print, for he hardly takes any part in the preparation of advertising or page layouts. Sometimes he can no longer recognize his photographs, for after they have been printed, the cropping and placement have given them a new significance. But it should not be a matter of indifference to a good photographer how illustrations are prepared. The reciprocal relationships of black, white and grey (color harmonies in a color photograph) are familiar to him; it should be an easy task for him to plan a well illustrated page himself after he has acquired the necessary knowledge.

The illustrator, too, generally regards his work as a self-sufficient entity; he expects his work will evoke the appreciation of typographers, make-up men and compositors, without his having to express any opinions other than platitudes about it. The art work, however, is dependent on the copy, so artists should be given (and take) every opportunity to learn themselves all the techniques by which their work will be laid out and printed.

The typographer's work is to develop the text layout in coordination with the typesetter. The typographer designs with typographic means. The illustration presented to him has a character of its own, and ignorance of this character can lead him to make mistakes of a technical kind or errors concerned with taste. It is thus essential for him to become familiar with the problems of form involved in the picture so that he can deal with and arrange the type correctly. The same applies to the compositor, who often carries out creative layout work.

The last member of the team is the art editor. The ultimate success of an advertisement (or a publication) depends very strongly on the make-up of pages. Each photograph and each drawing confronts us with problems of size, position and cropping. The choice, size and placement of the type can enhance or destroy the effectiveness of the printed piece.

The graphic arts obtain recruits from many quarters. If they come from editing or journalism, they usually lack knowledge of good photographic and pictorial design. If they come from the ranks of the photographers or commercial artists, they need more running acquaintance with type and its character so that they can find satisfactory and practical solutions. Unfortunately, journalism schools, technical schools and universities still concern themselves far too little with the problems of visual presentation. Their work in the training of editors, journalists, photographers, advertising specialists and commercial artists, becomes more important when it includes training in layout.

In book production, too, illustration is taking on an increasingly important rôle. Every book designer today must be versed in the foundations of make-up for illustrated pages. The possibilities of illustration in books are many: they range from the decorated initial and vignette through the drawn illustration and the "cut-in" photograph up to the illustrated book and the picture book. A book with full-page plates, containing only captions as text, is at the opposite pole from the book of yesteryear, comprised only of text for reading. In the picture book, layout is all-important, and decoration unnecessary. Every member of the layout team should therefore make himself familiar at least with the technical foundations of the other facets.

TASTE

Equally important are the demands of good taste, demands made on all professions concerned with pictures and writing. Advertising copywriters, artists, illustrators, photographers, typographers, editors and layout men exert an influence through their work on the taste of their fellow human beings. Their own sense of what is beautiful tends to become accepted as a standard by other people, and it must therefore be established without becoming crystallized into a rigid pattern. Every recruit to a field must be receptive to external influences, without abandoning himself to them. He should approach traditions with a critical eye and digest what is best, with the idea of transforming them and making them a part of his own mental property. Outright plagiarism can at best give only temporary success, for what is created by such means can never be vital, lively or well integrated.

Everyone concerned with the interplay of writing and pictures must know how to create functionally beautiful forms in a way that will make the right kind of appeal to the feelings. For if there are laws or formulae specifying the nature of beauty, they cannot be taught and learned. Like everything conceived by men, aesthetic principles cannot be eternally valid, and there are no laws of form which cannot be rejected by nature as often as they are confirmed. Just as existence itself conceals and reveals an infinity of possibilities, so the creation of graphic art, fortunately for its practitioners, has no visible boundaries. The real limits are not established by theories, commandments or prohibitions: they exist in ourselves. Good taste, if we have it, preserves us from offending, but it cannot be dictated by dogma.

The rules, challenges and advice which are offered and discussed in this book are simply facts of experience acquired from years of practice. If they are observed and used correctly, you are on the right path. But it will not be until the technical elements have become part of your flesh and blood, not until you can make your way forward without having to wonder which direction you should take, that you can consider yourself wholly dedicated to the pursuit of good design.

The unity of illustration and writing is too young a concept to have had classical exponents. There were great achievements in past centuries—the work of Gutenberg, Garamond, Bodoni, Didot and William Morris are outstanding examples. But the needs and potentialities of our age are so much more richly diversified that the external images of

the old masters' works serve as a model less than their mental attitudes. The great men of those periods were men of *their* century and *their* environment. In their day, their achievements were up to date, even ahead of their time. The best of them still seem agelessly beautiful, while the atypical has become obsolete. We can acknowledge our inheritance despite our natural urge to follow the currents of our age, despite our feeling that we must create something all our own. Tradition is two-sided: it can act as a strong support and give moderation to the strong, but it sometimes hampers the weak in their effort to reach new goals.

To place all one's faith in modernity requires strength of mind and spirit, for unsound influences lurk everywhere in books, periodicals, advertising literature, and shop windows. The currents of fashion are always short-lived. It is no easy matter to separate what is enduring and valuable from what is fleeting and transitory, and to develop it further. What appears extraordinary today becomes commonplace tomorrow, and loses all its charm a few days afterwards, because something still newer once again sweeps away yesterday's last word. The better—often of course merely the apparently better, because it is not visually hackneyed or threadbare—drives out the good. The vanguard in every field hastens to give concrete form to the unusual, without wondering how much of what seems so marvellously new is going to survive and endure. Revolutionaries often go astray, for they forge paths into unknown territory. What is really usable in experiments of pioneers is never lost, but enters into the consciousness of posterity and inspires its efforts. Even if we lack the courage or the imagination to work in the vanguard of a profession, we can keep our eyes on the pacesetters, the people who create the new foundations that allow the mainstream to be "modern."

It is essential for successful work, therefore, to examine constantly and critically new printed matter of every kind as well as the standard works on typography, graphic art, and the other arts, including architecture. Often, the discoveries we make will be of a negative kind, but there are lessons to be learned even in the worst examples.

Always examine the work done by others to see how it could be improved, and compare your own efforts with it. In all creative work, your critical gaze should never be obscured by your own achievements. If a student can find nothing wrong with his own work (when he takes another look at it after having left it alone for a time), he is stagnating and is in danger of lagging behind the mainstream, for time irrevocably changes all things. Success is reserved for those who can glimpse the path of progress, especially for those who are prepared to follow it.

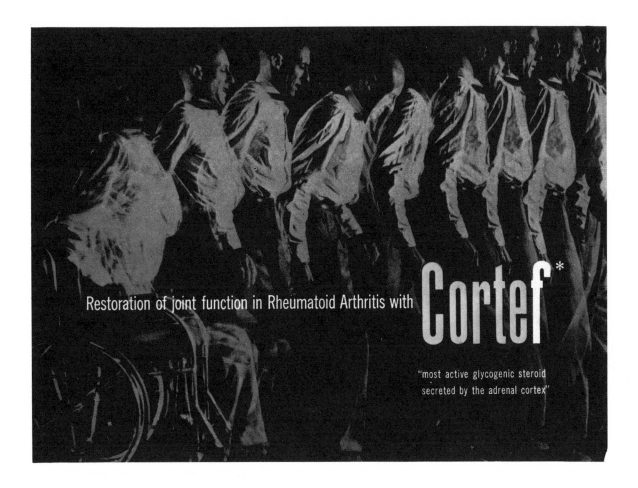

Illus. 1—The photographed movements of a convalescent printed in overlapping series provide a striking advertisement for a medicine. The dramatic effect is enhanced by the upward-striving outlines of the shirt creases in the series of pictures and by the profile, which grows progressively brighter. The white type on the dark blue ground seems to advance in support of the patient's efforts. At the end, like an exclamation, is the name of the health-giving preparation. Its first five letters are bright red, while the last letter is in white. This striking division of color recurs in the packages and in the other advertising used for the product.

Type

To ATTEMPT to deal with printing type as a cultural and historical phenomenon would make this book burst at its seams. The subject is interesting here merely because type acts as a means of expression, as a mediator between the writer and the reader. Handwriting is limited more to a private sphere: it no longer plays any rôle in business. Writing, therefore, is considered predominantly for our purposes as typesetting—supplemented of course by hand-drawn scripts, an accessory that allows the graphic artist to use a more personal approach than he can achieve with typefaces alone.

In 1440, Johann Gutenberg of Mainz invented the casting of separate letters in matrices struck from punches, setting type with these letters, as well as the hand press for movable type and printing of set-up texts on sheets of paper. Before Gutenberg's time every book had to be written by hand, or reproduced from a block or a woodcut—an engraved board. In principle, Gutenberg's method has remained unchanged to the present day, even though machine-typesetting, photo-composition, offset lithography and other printing processes which do not rely on printing direct from type have come into use.

The invention of letterpress printing brought an end to the Middle Ages. Reading and writing became every man's right; forms of type became more varied; hand-written letters were adapted and developed into new typefaces that conformed to the spirit of the age and its style of art.

The West knows two great type-groups: the Antiqua or Latin and the "Text"—Old English, Gothic or Black Letter. Each of them is subdivided into many families, which sometimes have no clearly defined boundaries

between them. In addition, there are other types which cannot be fitted into this simple scheme, because they have been designed on lines other than historical ones.

The development of typefaces which are of interest for us began in ancient Rome. Roman script was written in capital letters, its basic forms being developed from the square, the triangle and the circle. The large letters, the old Roman capitals, when reduced to skeleton form, and enriched by the later arrivals—G, J, K, U, W, X, Y and Z—have a unique, attractive rhythm of their own, no matter how they are composed in linear form. Because the distances between the letters in a given word vary, there is sometimes a layout problem. For example, the word "HIM" needs more space between letters than the word "ROOM" does. The words have to be "equalized"—letters must be separated from each other visually, not mathematically or mechanically. Type is said to be "letterspaced" when words are extended by *uniform* widening of the intervals, in order to make the word or line particularly striking. Yet, equal letterspacing is not always a solution for the layout man—hand-spacing may become necessary.

By Gutenberg's time, a large number of new scripts had evolved from the Roman capitals. The Roman capital script, originally used only by stonemasons, was written daily on wax tablets and became adapted more and more to the writing instrument used, the stylus, and the speed it could achieve. Capital script therefore became more and more "stenographized."

When the reed pen came into use later, and with it papyrus and parchment as writing materials, "rustic" capitals were employed. Generally they were slanted because of the speed at which they could thus be written. The rustic letters "ran" (Latin *currere*, "to run") so script typefaces which imitate handwriting are sometimes called "cursive." They are the source of the types now known as "*italic*" ("Italian"), because the first version was created by a Venetian printer, Aldus Manutius in 1501 for his "Aldine Press."

The script of the early Christian era was the "uncial," which developed from a rounding-off of the antique forms. Neither the rustic nor the uncial scripts used small letters, but an attempt was made to increase the legibility of the separate letters by the use of "ascenders" and "descenders"—the portions of the letters that rise or fall above or below the lines of the type body. The "half uncial" forms were developed from the uncials and Roman scripts. These were the first to vary capitals (majuscules) with small letters (minuscules).

When science flourished under the rule of Charlemagne, *circa* A.D. 800, and as men became increasingly concerned with preserving and making the best possible use of the written word, some form of letter was needed that could be easily written and read. A script was developed from uncials and half uncials containing both straight and rounded forms in rich variety. It could be written easily and rapidly with a quill pen. This lower-case script is the Carolingian minuscule. It has hardly changed to the present day and has become the handwriting of the Western world.

The Romance and Gothic ages were of course not without influence upon the forms of letters; these became pointed, broken, slender. Thus Text, Black Letter and various intermediate and mixed forms arose.

The classification of typefaces is a matter to which type designers, engravers, printers, publishers and scientific experts have devoted

their attention through the centuries with varying degrees of success. No one system has been found despite efforts to arrive at a universally acceptable and systematic classification. A similar situation occurred in classifying art: the same styles and periods have been given widely divergent names, which are either misleading or make unclear distinctions.

Without going into great detail, we can classify the typefaces used today as follows:

Among the rounded types which have developed out of the ancient Roman capitals and the Carolingian minuscule letters are families of type which are themselves subdivided into classes.

The first family, Roman typefaces (mostly with serifs), has three classes.

1. Venetian, less appropriately but traditionally known as "Mediaeval." Representative of this class are the types of Claude Garamond, Aldus Manutius and Nicolas Jenson, originally used in the 15th and 16th centuries. The capital letters in the first texts of this period are reproductions of the Roman stone inscriptions with their horizontal linear arms, originally formed in stone by the mason's chisel. The feet, crosslines and serifs were added in the 9th century to the small letters which came into use at that time; these had developed from the strokes made with an obliquely held quill pen. The minuscules thus stood on horizontal feet, while the upper strokes were slanting and the loops of the letters had their strongest point not in the vertical but—following the way the broad quill was held—in the diagonal from the lower left-hand side to the upper right.

2. Old-Face Roman is the connecting link with Modern Roman types, and arose in the Baroque period. The most important examples were the types of Anton Janson, William

Illus. 2—The letter "n" in seven variations of rounded typefaces. nnnnnnn

Left to right: Renaissance Roman (also known as Mediaeval), Old Style Roman, Modern Roman, Sans Serif or Grotesque, Egyptienne, Italienne and Clarendon.

Caslon, John Baskerville and Pierre Fournier, leading with a reinforcement of the contrast between stems and hairlines to the still more varied forms which developed from the copperplate (no longer from the broad quill!).

3. Modern Face, the Roman form of neoclassical type used in the Empire and Victorian periods. Its chief representative was Giambattista Bodoni (1740–1813), who printed mainly in Italy and gave this period its "typical" pattern. The Didot family in France and Walbaums in Germany were other important creators of typefaces in this period.

Varieties of these Roman forms arose in the early decades of the 19th century as a result of the longing of that period for what was new and different. Many of these variants disappeared almost immediately after their first appearance, others maintained their existence and are still alive today, transformed and adapted to modern taste.

So there arose a large family of Linear typefaces, known in printing as Gothic, Grotesque, Egyptienne, Italienne and Clarendon. The names have no connections with the characters of the typefaces; they are born from fantasy.

The first class of Linear typefaces includes the Sans Serif Roman forms, whose uniformly thick lines reflect the skeleton forms of the Roman. They were written or drawn with a round-tipped pen. The form called "Grotesque" by printers is sometimes designated as a "block letter."

The second class of Linear typefaces (uniformly thick or almost uniformly thick types) has serifs. The Egyptienne forms have serifs in the same thickness as the connecting lines, placed on the verticals without any rounding-off. The Continental Italienne (not to be confused with the slanting Italic types), which is legible and aesthetically tolerable only in isolated words, has strong horizontal lines and heavy serifs, but slender verticals. Clarendon, developed primarily in England, differs from Egyptienne by the clear distinction between hairlines and stems. The heavy serifs of the hairlines are rounded off.

The cursive typefaces developed out of the written scripts of the Renaissance humanists and in the chancelleries of the spiritual and temporal lords. Only a few of these types have developed independently—most of them are variants of a basic typeface family. They thus serve mainly as supplementary and distinguishing types in the large section of the rounded (Roman) typefaces.

In book printing, it is mainly the Roman forms with serifs which are used—both the historical kinds and the newly developed ones—while advertising prefers to use the Linear varieties, which have a more challenging appearance. Used as letterpress types in catalogues, brochures or trade folders, etc., small typefaces of the Linear kind (Grotesques) tend to fatigue the eyes more quickly.

The broken typefaces, the Gothic or Black Letter, are being driven more and more to the wall by the modern trend of our age away from nationalism. This is regrettable, for many of these letters are beautifully formed.

At the time of Gutenberg, around the middle of the 15th century, Text or Narrow Black Letter was in use. The curves of the small letters were broken, and the type image came to resemble a tapestry. Round Black Letter was less vertically emphasized, with a lighter and looser image than Text.

Graphic artists have been busying themselves since the beginning of the 20th century with the design of new typefaces, which bear more or less clearly the mark of the artist's personality. They are either remodellings of old typefaces or they strike out on entirely new paths. Many of them have proved in the course of the years to be as vital as the old ones, while others have quickly disappeared because they were merely fashionable. The names given by the type foundries to these types are usually chosen on account of their classification rather than their advertising effectiveness.

THE TYPOGRAPHIC SYSTEM

Gutenberg and his successors knew neither a uniform system of measurement nor a standard size and height for typefaces. Firmin Didot (1764–1836) introduced the method of typographic measurement generally used today except in Great Britain and the United States, which adopted a modification of Didot's "point" system in the late 19th century.

Everyone concerned with type and printing should be thoroughly familiar with the point system. The standard Anglo-American typographical point measures 1/72 of an inch (0.013837 in.). A "pica" is 1/6 of an inch or 12 points, so that an inch has 72 points. The square frame of any type size is called an "em," and the em of 12-point or pica type is used to measure the widths of columns: a line of 9-point type 2 inches or 12 picas (144 points) wide contains 16 ems, and a 6-point line of the same width 24 ems.

Non-printing material used in composing includes spaces for separating letters or words; the leads (pronounced "leds," not "leeds") or spacelines which establish the distance between lines; and the "furniture" (wooden bars and blocks) which hold the printed matter in place and serve as "blind" material where large white spaces are required.

If the text lines are separated from each other only by the point size of the types, i.e., without leading, it is called "solid." Solid matter is used in the printing of the text of some books, magazines and newspapers. When the text is to be given more breathing-space—usually to make it more legible—it must be spaced by hand with thin strips of lead if more than three points is needed; the machines which set the type can set the body larger than the face by one point to three points easily—so that 8 point on 10 point body is common, as is 12 point on 15 point body.

Non-standard typefaces rich in contrasts and intended to attract attention are used mainly in advertising.

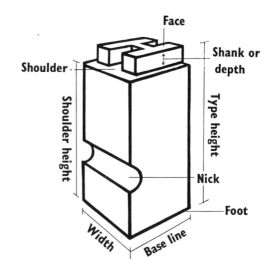

Illus. 4—The lead letters are set in the composing stick by the hand-setter from left to right, but upside down, each line adjoining the previous one. The nick, a groove in the side of the body, enables the typesetter to place the letters in correct position even without looking at them. Nicks in different forms and heights differentiate types and variants of basic typeface forms from each other. Italic letters sometimes have projections, called "kerns," so that they can be placed close together: the overhanging kern rests on the shoulder of the preceding type just as the descender lies on the shoulder of the letter below.

For solid and machine-leaded matter, it is sufficient to specify the type, its size, the length of the line and the depth of the matter, while the make-up of a display-type text must be prepared so that the compositor can work in accordance with a layout.

To do its job effectively, every piece of printed matter must be suited for its specific purpose. The selection of type and its arrange-

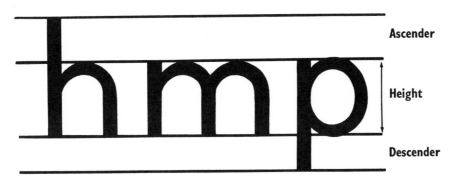

Illus. 3

ment on paper must be made primarily with this in view.

In most cases the rectangular form of the paper determines the shape of what is to be printed on it: lines almost always run parallel to the edges of the paper, no matter whether they are to be read from left to right as in the Western world, or from right to left as in the East. Obliquely placed blocks of matter or isolated lines introduce an alien element into the whole, are disquieting and should be used with caution. Restless movements of such a kind should always be caught up again by horizontal lines.

The type area must be well proportioned in relation to the edges of the paper. The open spaces, especially the borders of the paper, are just as important for a good appearance as the printed area is. Legibility and the best use of available materials are decidedly important. Apart from them, there is the question of advertising value—whether reserve is called for or an eye-catching effect is aimed at. There is no absolute standard of measurement: each element obtains its effect only by its relationship to the others. A pica-size line on a business card has a different effect from the same line on a large magazine page.

Most suitable for the text of periodicals, catalogues and folders are the 6-point to 12-point sizes of types (6, 6½, 7, 8, 9, 10, 11 and 12) whose baselines, serifs, ascenders and descenders are well balanced, and are not too much at variance in their relative strengths. Types and spacing must give a uniformly silver-grey picture. Excessively powerful faces tire the eyes after long reading; and Grotesque types, lacking the fine nuances of the serifs, should also be used with caution in long texts.

Lengthy texts are best set in 9-point to 12-point types, leaded 2 points to make them more legible.

Solid matter, especially in long lines (26 picas or more), is also tiring. Bold-face types can take strong spacing in order to reinforce the horizontal movement still more, though the lines must then be correspondingly long to allow this emphasis to become effective. Your eye and sense of form are decisive for determining measurements. In spaced texts, above all in documents, diplomas, etc., with capital letters, the space between lines must always be optically bigger than the space between words, and the space between words must be greater than normal when space between lines is three points or more. Prepare your typographical order with full specifications as to spacing.

The choice of types available from printers is generally very large. The question of which to use is decided by the kind of work to be done and the layout man's personal inclinations. The type should correspond to the spirit of the advertisement: for literature dealing with heavy industries, solid, simple forms are advisable, while the world of fashion demands light, vivacious types. Many types provide in themselves such an attractive and well-balanced picture that they remain effective in indifferent layouts, while other kinds are so aggressive that they prove fit for advertising layouts only if they are skilfully handled.

Type foundries and many printers make suggestions in their sample books to help the work of clients and layout men.

Obviously the typefaces used for body matter can also be employed for captions and other distinctive portions. Many types have variants which differ from the normal form by having stronger lines or varying serifs, oblique, italic, script, bold, shaded or outline. These co-ordinated and mutually complementary type forms are called the alternate fonts of a type family. They serve — singly, mixed or in their totality—to enliven printed matter. If you need emphasis or contrast in a book or an advertisement, it is always a good idea to seek it first in the fonts of *one* type form, so that all the forms of the letters will harmonize with each other.

The choice of a distinctive type which diverges altogether from the basic depends on the principle of emphasized contrasting effects. But caution is advisable so that powerfully varying characteristics will not conflict with one another. Renaissance Roman types (evolved from writing done with a broad quill pen) should never be mixed with the forms of the neo-classical Roman (derived from copper-plate engraving, and thus more artificial)

No messy ice trays

créations

KIOWA MOON
FRESH HOME-COOKED TASTE

Million END

the new miracle fabrics

The 'copters are coming

How long since you've taste

OVERSTOLZ

Preferred for flavor far above all other margarines!

Illus. 5—Hand lettering, because of its individuality, gives animation to a page of printed matter.

forms. Suitable for both, however, are Linear type forms if used for purposes of distinction (not vice versa). In the case of script and cursive forms, observe carefully whether they are derived from the brush or from the broad or narrow pen. They suit correspondingly-designed typefaces. If two slanted types are used together, their degree of inclination must be identical.

Most types gain their effect principally from lively alternation of large and small letters. Lines in all capitals appear quiet and distinguished, but are often difficult to read, especially in long words or headlines, because of the uniformity of the letters.

In spite of the wealth of beautifully designed types available, hand lettering by an artist has substantial value in advertising for a particular purpose. For a headline whose meaningfulness depends on the unique rhythm of its sequence of letters, or for a line with individual letters co-ordinated as they can never be in ordinary set type, or for a hint of self-assertiveness or freedom inside a word or a line, the custom-designed product is easy to distinguish from the best assortment of ready-made types.

Drawn and written types for different duties are shown in Illustrations 5 and 6. Their vitality and individuality cannot be matched by composed types. Their special character helps to make a piece of printed matter immediately recognizable as belonging to a particular enterprise.

PLACING TYPE ON THE PAGE

Generally, paper or a similar substance is the "stock" that carries print. In planning books, magazines and self-contained advertisements (catalogues, price lists, leaflets, brochures, business literature, posters and ephemeral literature) size is the first thing that must be decided. Like the choice of paper, size is determined by the purpose of the printed matter and the work it is expected to do.

Where is the block of text to be located on the size of paper selected? The most obvious place is in the middle; and this may do very well for a single sheet, provided it is the optical middle and not the geometrical middle. If you put the block of text on your paper so that the white spaces above and below are measurably equal, the text will "droop." It will appear, in fact, to lie below the middle. It must therefore be pushed up until you have the feeling that it is just right.

In all creative work, measurements judged by the eye are more reliable than those arrived at with a ruler, for the reader's reaction will also be the product of his feelings. The eye for which you are creating your layout can easily be deceived. You must always make allowances for this quite justifiable deception in all your calculations. You will acquire from experience a sense of aesthetic fitness and a feeling for proportion, especially if you study carefully the examples that follow.

If a printed area looks unsymmetrical on its paper background, equalization must be found which will level off the asymmetry and thus "pacify" the page—and its reader.

Every tension needs a compensating relaxation if it is not to cause discomfort, but a complete lack of tension brings tedium in its train. Every well-done piece of work is a balance of stresses and reliefs. There are both traditional and novel ways of ensuring that this equilibrium is achieved. We must search unceasingly—in advertising most of all—for new ways of effective expression.

Wide margins give distinction to a text, particularly when the matter is printed in large-size type and is strongly leaded out. The commonest use of such layouts is in documents, diplomas and picture books.

In a book, apart from its title page, no single page can be judged on its own merits: the open double page is the graphic unity. The inner sides of left-hand and right-hand pages are generally closer to the middle after binding "take-in" is considered. Formulae have been drawn up for the proportions discovered by Gutenberg, Aldus Manutius, Didot, Bodoni and other old masters of book design. These specifications are that the length of the line should be two-thirds of the width of the paper, and that width-ratios of 2:3:4:5, 2:3:4:6 or 2:3:5:6 are most pleasing for the inside, top, outside and bottom margins respectively. Such

9 out of 10 Screen Stars

More people own
Toastmaster Toasters
than any other kind

Cleaner, Fresher Complexion
Why show your age? You don't tell it!

Monolog am Strand

Spring came to a broker

Tabasco - a Tradition of Fine Dining the World Over

Pfau Krawatten vorbildlich

Illus. 6—Most written types have developed from handwriting, and therefore have a personal and intimate appearance. Brush-written scripts are popular in America and elsewhere.

Illus. 7—Interesting arrangements of columns on a double page. No. 1 shows the blocks of text in their traditional relationship: the inside margin is 2 units, the top margin 3 units, the outside margin 4 units and the bottom margin 5 or 6 units. The width of the text corresponds to two thirds of the width of the page. In No. 3, the page may appear crowded as the paper is almost entirely utilized. The effects in Nos. 4, 5 and 6 result from the contrast between printed and unprinted areas.

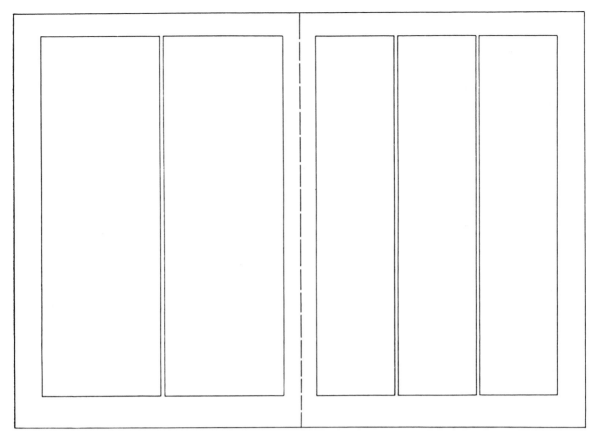

Illus. 8—Two-column and three-column division of a page. The optimal reading width of a line is 50 to 55 letters, which corresponds to a line 12 or 13 picas long for 6-point type, 15 or 16 picas for 8-point type, 17 or 18 picas for 9-point, and 19 or 20 picas for 10-point. With 12-point and larger, lines of 24 to 30 picas are often used in books. Always leave a point between lines and more leading for lines of more than 16 picas. Shorter lines than 12 picas, sometimes used in newspaper copy, disturb the reading rhythm and are also unattractive because of the many necessary hyphenations and the unequal distances between words.

a mathematically determined relationship should, however, always be merely the starting point towards a final decision on the placement of blocks of text for each particular case.

To obtain the final measurements, place on a sheet of paper of the same size as the double page, two pieces of light grey paper corresponding to the text matter in size. Better still use two blocks of proofs showing the type spaced out as it has been chosen for printing. Your printer will be able to supply proofs for these experiments. Move the sheets about until you find the most appropriate and visually attractive position.

In these experiments, it will be found that out-of-the-way, unsymmetrical layouts can be quite effective, especially for advertising. But unusual designs should not be elevated to the status of universally applicable rules, for unusualness tends to prove fatiguing over the long run and weaker than layouts which adhere to tradition. Single books or series of volumes, periodicals, etc., which contain long masses of solid text are usually less tiring to read when the eye and brain have to concern themselves only with the tension contained in the text itself and its meaning. If your page layout is anything but simple, it will distract the reader. The more extensive a piece of advertising matter is, too, the more sparingly you should use any fireworks in the form of startlingly novel ideas.

A text consisting only of equally long lines seems overpowering if there are no "breathing spaces" in it. It *must* therefore be subdivided into paragraphs and sections, perhaps with subheads. The quiet contours of a page of text

Illus. 9—Various arrangements of type blocks. (1) Lines in block format with flush paragraphs. (2) Block format with indented paragraphs. (3) Lines flush on left and "ragged" or "rough" on the right, as in typewritten material, are used primarily for poems and plays. (4) The rarely used system with flush lines on the right, rough on the left. (5) Centred or mid-line format: the parts of the matter are symmetrically arranged. This is used chiefly in book title pages and documents, sometimes also for poetry. (6) A mobile line arrangement: the lines are broken and placed in verbal and graphic patterns, a lively arrangement.

or of a column of type are best preserved when the beginnings and ends of paragraphs are incomplete lines. Except in advertising, no new paragraph should be unindented, i.e., flush with the left-hand margin, but no indention should be longer than a quarter of a line's length, or it will disturb the harmony of the page. If extra spaces are inserted between paragraphs, they will often impair the rhythm of the lines. Instead of indenting, you can separate paragraphs by "paragraph starters," "¶" or other symbols, or by "bullets" (large

points) or asterisks in the text to avoid destroying the uniform outlines of a column.

Page (folio) numbers and also "running" heads can be designed to belong to the column. Column headings are used primarily in books and large catalogues, placed inside the type area, but set in a smaller size of the basic type, or in small capitals. Although generally at the top, there is no standardized position for them. They can be placed either in the middle or, better still, underneath the outer edge of the type area. As for the folios, they are customarily

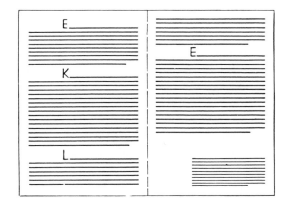

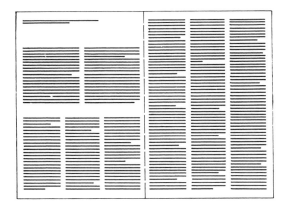

Illus. 10—Matter in various column-widths enlivens pages of solid text, but this should be done only when it is justifiable for practical reasons. Alternating sizes of type and space between lines in groups of text enable varying effects of grey to be achieved. In composing magazines, newspapers, and advertising literature on a larger scale, moderate use of these variations prevents the reader's eye from being tired by a uniform text.

on the same line as the running heads but kept to the outside.

In body type—and in every other kind of printed matter—purity of style should always be aimed at. Asymmetrical text layouts should never be mixed with symmetrical ones in the same work. This is a mistake often made in books and advertising literature.

Chapters are major divisions of text. Designing their beginnings with distinctive characteristics and headings is among the most rewarding planning tasks for creators and layout men because these can be used to relieve the uniformity of solid text matter. The beginnings of books and chapters can also be indicated by decorative letters (initials), a line of capitals or a word in capitals and small capitals. Naturally the form of the beginnings of chapters must be the same throughout the whole work. This applies to other subdivisions as well.

So that pages register (line up) well with their reverse sides and facing pages, empty spaces must exactly correspond, or be "justified," and the text matter must be exactly the same length and width. Proper alignment between lines of type and on a line is called "justification."

The most suitable width for the text depends on the size of the type used. If 6-point lines are more than 20 picas wide they are hard to read, especially when unleaded or with only small leading. If the type area is wider than 30 picas, it can advantageously be divided into two columns (with one pica or more between) if the basic type is not larger than 10-point.

CALCULATING THE MANUSCRIPT

All text to be set up should first be clearly and neatly typewritten on one side of a sheet of paper. It is only possible to make an unquestionably accurate calculation of the length of the text—and subsequently to order type composition that can be executed without any trouble—if there is a neat copy of the manuscript to work from.

Exact instructions for composition and make-up should always be attached to it. These instructions should contain all the information needed regarding typeface, size of type, length of line, leading, indentions, type area, size of paper, margins, treatment of beginnings of chapters or sections, any special typefaces or sizes, treatment of headings, footnotes, tables, table of contents, design of the title page, and any other relevant data.

You can calculate the average number of letters on a page of typescript by pencilling two long vertical lines along the right-hand side of a typed page, one line joining the final characters of the longest lines, the other passing through the final characters of the shortest lines (ignoring the ends of paragraphs). Then draw a third line down the middle of the first two. Count the number of typed characters from the left side in this "standard" or average line; include in your count the spaces between words; then multiply this figure by the number of lines on the typed page. (Count the final lines at the end of a paragraph as complete lines, as it is better to allow too much space than too little.)

Example: the average line has 61 characters and the whole page 43 lines. The page therefore has 2,623 letters. If the number of letters and lines on the other typescript pages is the same, subsequent calculation of the whole text is easy. Otherwise the total number of lines on each page in the typescript must be multiplied out.

If a whole text has, let us say, 121 pages with 45 lines of 64 letters each, the typescript contains $121 \times 2,880 = 348,480$ letters. A paper is chosen measuring $5\frac{3}{4} \times 8\frac{1}{4}$ inches. The type area is 26 picas wide by 38 picas (approximately $4\frac{3}{8} \times 6\frac{3}{8}$ inches) deep. The type used is Bodoni Roman 9-point, with 3-point leading, for a total depth of 12 points per line. In counting out 5 lines of text, which the printer has supplied as a pattern, it is confirmed that on an average 72 letters fit in the width of 26 picas. Each page with 38 lines (that fit into 38 picas) contains 38×72 (or 2,736) letters. Divide 2,736 into the solid matter of 348,480 letters and you will find that you need just less than 128 pages. (Actually, the page will be 3 points short of 38 picas as there are 37 spaces between the 38 lines—for a total of 453 points.)

If the same text were set solid in 9-point, there would be room for 50 lines on an almost equally deep page of 450 points. The 50 lines of 72 letters per line would give 3,600 letters per page. So, 348,480 divided by 3,600 would come to about 98 pages.

If the text is subdivided into chapters, each chapter must be calculated separately if it begins on a fresh page. If you plan each chapter to begin on a new right-hand page, you can adjust easily the differences which are bound to appear even when counting is correctly done, because at best, calculation of typed script into type-set is approximate. Corrections that may be necessary after the page proofs have been supplied will then be easier to make.

To the total of text pages you have to add the pages for the title, table of contents, index and other special information, as well as the blank sheets customarily provided at the front and back of the book.

If you have to make a calculation based on a given size for a book, and the above-mentioned amount of text is to be used, you proceed as follows:

The extent of the work is to be about 112 pages (7 signatures or "sections," each 16 pages). The book begins with a blank leaf (pages 1 and 2). Page 3 contains the main title; on page 4 is the copyright notice. The actual text will begin on page 7, and it must end at the latest on page 108. The reason is that two pages must be left in front for the table of contents and two pages at the back for the index. At the end, just as at the front, you want to leave two blank pages. There are thus not more than 102 pages available for the actual text.

The printer offers Garamond in 8-, 9-, 10- and 12-point sizes. The 12-point size is too large, the 8-point size too small for such a large body of text. The 9-point size is preferable to the 10-point, which would probably have to be set solid. If therefore we choose 9-point with 2-point spacing, 41 lines of 9-point on 11 will be produced with a page depth of about 38 picas. So, 41×11 points $= 451$ points, minus 2 points for the last spaceline $= 449$ points. A 26-pica long 9-point line of Garamond contains 77 letters; the page thus has $77 \times 41 = 3,157$ letters. Therefore, 348,480 typescript characters divided by 3,157 letters in the text per page indicates a little more than 110 pages. This exceeds the stipulated size by almost a tenth. The 11-point high lines (9 points and 2 points space) must therefore be reduced by a tenth. To use 9-point type with 1-point spacing will leave room for 45 lines per page, or 3,465 letters. Now, 348,480 divided by 3,465 = 101 pages. You have a choice either of letting the text begin on page 7 half-way down the page with an initial (so that part of page 108 will contain text), or of using page 108 as a blank page facing the index. (Remember, this example book is not chapterized.)

If calculations show an excess or a deficit, there are various possibilities for adjustment: size of type, spacing, length of line (width of text) or column or page depth can be changed. When the type is set by hand, the leading can be altered, but in machine-set type this is difficult if the spacing is decided on before the type is set and the leading was cast immediately with the type on a larger body. Afterwards, the spacing can only be increased, and by hand.

If, for a chapterized book, exact data as to type size and width can be decided in advance, it will suffice in the case of solid setting to leave page make-up to the compositor, and simply to order spacing for adjustment later, when page proofs are available. Occasionally, however, it is better to paste-up the galley proofs oneself into a page dummy. This is particularly important when illustrations are to be inserted or tables and footnotes to be correctly placed. For pasting-up pages it is best to use a double-page ruled dummy, so you can see the facing type areas.

Size calculations are part of the ABC of every layout man; constant practice will enable you to acquire dexterity.

Another task: a manuscript has 5 chapters, and each chapter is to start on a new sheet, i.e., on a new right-hand page. The chapters begin, however, one-third of the way down the page. The top third of the page is intended for the chapter head. It is intended that there shall be a blank sheet at the beginning and end of the volume. The half title, title page and table of contents each need one page, the index 5 pages.

The typescript has 46 lines on every full page.

The lines average 70 characters. Thus, each full page has 3,220 letters.

Chapter 1, 25 full pages plus page with 14 lines = 81,480 letters

Chapter 2, 36 full pages plus page with 20 lines = 117,320 letters

Chapter 3, 47 full pages plus page with 4 lines = 151,620 letters

Chapter 4, 41 full pages plus page with 19 lines = 133,350 letters

Chapter 5, 71 full pages plus page with 18 lines = 229,880 letters

The size of the book is $5\frac{1}{2} \times 8\frac{1}{4}$ inches, the type area 24 picas wide and about 38 picas deep. A 10-point type size with 3-point spacing has been chosen. Calculating 35 lines of 13-points makes 455 points, almost exactly 38 picas. A line width of 24 picas needs 62 letters or 2,170 letters to a page of text. As 12 lines (a trifle less than one-third) are omitted on the first page of each chapter (for "sinkage"), their 744 letters must be added to the length of the 5 chapters.

Chapter 1—81,480 plus 744 =
  82,224 divided by 2,170 =
  37 pages and 32 lines or 38 pages

Chapter 2—117,320 plus 744 =
  118,064 divided by 2,170 =
  54 pages and 15 lines or 55 pages

Chapter 3—151,620 plus 744 =
  152,364 divided by 2,170 =
  70 pages and 8 lines or 71 pages

Chapter 4—133,350 plus 744 =
  134,094 divided by 2,170 =
  61 pages and 28 lines or 62 pages

Chapter 5—229,880 plus 744 =
  230,624 divided by 2,170 =
  106 pages and 10 lines or 107 pages

This necessitates the following page arrangement:

		1 blank page
blank page	2	3 half title (or colophon)
blank page	4	5 title page
copyright notice	6	7 table of contents
blank page	8	9 1st chapter begins
1st chapter ends	46	47 2nd chapter begins
		101 2nd chapter ends
blank page	102	103 3rd chapter begins
		173 3rd chapter ends

The extent of the work is 352 pages or 22 signatures of 16 pages. Chapters 2, 3 and 5 end on a right-hand page, so that the following left-hand page remains blank.

TYPOGRAPHICAL DRAWING

As a general rule, pages containing pure text can be planned without any extensive dummying or drawing. Only pages to be set up by hand or those with a complicated structure—title pages, tables, tables of contents, indexes, etc.—need be presented in the form of exact drawings. Display type, however, always needs a layout.

The most important aids in drawing are pencils of varying grades of hardness. It is an advantage, however, to know how to write the basic forms of the Western letters with a lettering pen. Knowledge of the skeleton form makes it easier to draw type. In addition to pencils, you will need for typographical drawing a carpenter's pencil, colored pencils, a ruler, a typographic rule of metal, or better still of celluloid graduated in inches, picas and points (6, 7, 8, 9 and 10 points), erasers, strong tracing paper and smear-proof writing or drawing paper. For drawing skeleton type, you need lettering pens of varying sizes and India ink, along with narrowly lined or squared paper (quadrille paper). Because of the typographic point system used it is advisable to obtain paper with pica divisions (each square 1/6 inch). If you get accustomed to working on a drawing board with a T-square and set square (triangle), you will be able to draw in right angles anywhere you need them and will thereby have an advantage, particularly in the exact calculation of picture sizes and cuts. But even when the layout man works without a drawing board his tools should include a right-angle triangle or set square.

Type sizes from 6 to 12 points should preferably be drawn as grey lines to produce the effect of the lines of type. The varying grey effect of the different types is obtained by drawing with correspondingly soft pencils. It is important that the tonal value should be correctly reproduced in your layout. Thin and light types, therefore, should be drawn with a hard pencil; strong and bold-face types with a soft one. In mixed text, the height of the em is indicated by the thickness of the line, as the few ascenders and descenders do not affect the dominant typographic color of the page. If capitals are used the line must of course be as high as the capital letters. In fixing the distance between the em-height and the em of the next line take care not to forget ascenders and descenders and the between-line spacing. If lengthy texts must be drawn for a final version, arrange just 3 or 4 lines, transfer them to the edge of a strip of paper (from which the measurements can be made) and then transfer by tracing preferably to the layout page.

If large sizes of type are to be used, it is best to draw letters separately. In advertisements or complicated work in which the position of each word is important, smaller type sizes than 12-point should also be sketched in the size of the letters.

If you have type samples available, begin by sketching the alphabet of a typeface in a large size, or trace it carefully on a piece of transparent paper so that you gain an idea of the thickness of the type's lines, its flow and its distinctive characteristics. But do not draw outlines and fill them in afterwards; it is best to use a pencil of the right hardness and to place pencil stroke against pencil stroke until the drawn letters have the appearance and thickness of the model. When study has made you familiar with the type and its forms, it will be easier for you to draw the type in other sizes too. For the height (ascenders, body-height and descenders) make your lines in light pencil. It is important to make a complete set of models (small and large alphabet, numbers, punctuation marks and other signs) for at least one size of all types with which you are going to work. Most printers will be glad to supply type samples. (If you make photostats you will not

ABCDEFGHIJKLMN
OPQRSTUVWXYZ
abcdefghijklm
nopqrstuvwxyz
1234567890

Illus. 11—Every layout man must be able to hand letter Roman type in its basic form as skeleton type, for it is the foundation of all layout work. Begin with a lettering pen and change later to a pencil or pointed pen when you have learned how to make the characters.

gain the practical skill needed.) The more carefully you indicate the main lines in a layout drawing, the easier it will be for your client and everyone else to gain an impression of the final appearance of the printed work.

The layout artist need not burden himself with seldom-used types, but should be fully capable of reproducing them from type specimen books. Persistence is more important than talent; drawing is a matter of practice and experience rather than of genius. The minimum requirement for unskilled artists is that even superficial indications of lines to be set or drawn must make the proportions of the whole layout recognizable. Above all, artists and compositors, as well as layout artists, should be familiar enough with typefaces to be able to create and read layouts so that no technical inquiries have to be made while work is in progress.

If you wish to draw negative type (white type on a black background, such as is often seen in advertisements) paint the surface with

India ink or, better still, use black paper cut to the appropriate size. The letters can then be drawn on it with chalk or with a pen or brush and opaque poster white.

If you can join a school course on type designing or typographical drawing, you should not fail to take the opportunity, for a chance to watch an expert at work is far more instructive than a textbook.

The development of new printing techniques and the changeover from hand-setting via the typesetting machine to photo-composition has given the type artist new aids, even if this does not always make him rejoice. Poster artists in particular now work with alphabets of rubber letters, using them to "print" extensive texts successfully on posters and placards. The result is a stipple-face, with a legibility that makes it effective, especially if Grotesque types are used.

Used in America, and increasingly in Europe too, are "Artype," "Letraset" and other alphabets in many shapes and sizes which can be cut out and attached to any surface, or

where do type ideas come from ?

LEE PAPER COMPANY

rubbed on like a decalcomania. Letters also can be purchased on colored adhesive foils and as screen patterns on cellophane. Many of these are informal-looking brush-types, which convey a personal note precisely because they do not have to stand "at attention." All of these are easily recognizable as ready-made because of the complete agreement between duplicates of the same letters, reminiscent of composed types. They cannot replace the work of a good typographic artist.

The illustrations in this book are occasionally drawn in India ink, not in pencil. This has been done to demonstrate the possibilities of line drawing, and also because a line plate usually reproduces the situation more strikingly than a halftone does.

To create something new, craftsmanship is necessary. For a good layout, you need not only a sense of form but also exact knowledge of the essential requirements in manual skill and technique. Calculation and type-drawing must be practised again and again. You will soon find it impossible to look at a layout without feeling compelled to form your own opinion of it. By its very existence, every piece of printed matter, regardless of whether it is good or bad, invites criticism. It is not only important to be able to recognize *whether* it is good or mediocre, but also *why* it is. The desire to make it better must follow naturally from the opinion you have formed, but the desire can only be successfully realized if you have developed a solid basis of good workmanship to draw on as well as good intentions. Complete familiarity with all the ideas in the section you have just read will give you a good start.

26

The Picture

THERE ARE two chief methods of pictorial representation: by photograph and by painted or drawn picture. Paintings and drawings are not always exact representations of concrete things. They are often the results, put into visible form, of moving experiences, and are not intended to be evaluated as descriptions but as expressions. The photograph, however, is nearly always a factual report, close to the reality of things. Sometimes it seems to break out of the narrow limits of practical attainment with a camera into other, broader, dimensions. While artists in oil and pencil can give form to their ideas only after painstaking work, the photographer can capture the picture before his eyes immediately and directly (although he may have spent hours preparing). Although the two forms of communication have much in common, they are necessarily judged in different ways, for they have their origin in different spheres of consciousness. Essential in both of them, however, is that power be gained when what is represented is offered in a concentrated form, free from accidental or irrelevant factors. The photograph always inclines more strongly to "reportage"—and this is a quality that often arouses an instinctive distaste when found in a painting. Even if the popular opinion that the camera cannot lie is very debatable, *belief* in its infallibility, and the speed of photographic reproduction, have made photography an unparalleled method for conveying information.

In the dawn of history, pictures and writing were one and the same; the picture is still "read" by the eye just as writing is. Letters themselves, after all, are the highly diagrammatic abstract forms of what were once pictorial representations, "pictographs."

Pictures have more potentialities for expression than writing: they range from naturalistic representation, the basic element of photography, right up to an abstract symbolism that can depict infinity or eternal recurrence by means of a circle. Advertising makes use of all these methods, photographic and artistic, to convey conviction.

With the invention of photography, the picture lost its rarity-value. Anyone who was technically expert enough could now make "real pictures"—their creation was no longer the prerogative of artists. In the course of its evolution, photography, like painting, has undergone many changes both with respect to choice of subject and to presentation. Today we are no longer bound by any kind of orthodoxy or by established techniques of exposure and developing: we gratefully accept anything of value wherever it is to be found.

THE PHOTOGRAPH

The photograph is our time's supreme form of self-expression: the growth of the pictorial sections in books, magazines and newspapers and the development of films and television demonstrate this fact. This development has brought a certain amount of over-simplification with it. The photograph is universally understandable and so appears not to need explanations to supplement it. Its power to convey experience increases as superfluous details are eliminated. It attains its highest potential when the representation becomes purely symbolic.

Whether the layout artist selects a drawing or a photograph depends on the task to be fulfilled and the purpose of the representation, but the basis of choice and judgment is the same. Each is most convincing precisely in that field which has been exclusively or at any rate predominantly assigned to it. In general,

27

drawings and paintings tend to be static—they depict an enduring condition. The very nature of the photograph is dynamic—it fixes movement, life, the fleeting moment. Each form of representation can of course complement the other, or both may be used together. The photograph is a report.

A good photographer influences the character of his work even while he is planning it. He directs his subject as much as he can, builds it up or transforms it in his mind, and strives, when it escapes his ability to change it, to choose the best location, the most promising time, the best lighting conditions, to obtain the desired result. It is essential that he know how to utilize the many aids which the photographic industry can offer him, and that his knowledge in this direction be just as extensive as his acquaintance with that other wide sector of his work that demands manual skill.

The direction of the light is all-important in portraits and photographs of objects: it can shape a subject, emphasize it or suppress it.

Nevertheless, it is the photographer's outlook and imagination that endow a picture with its unmistakable features. Many subjects are photographed again and again, particularly in regions popular among tourists. By making comparisons between the versions of the different photographers it is possible for you to evaluate them—judge by the degree of intensification of natural qualities which make a good picture. Other series of variations on a single pictorial theme can be collected for criticism from magazines, tourist folders and postcards. Note what advantages one has over another and which particular small details add to the value of a picture or distract the eye. In making such judgments it is of course an advantage if you take the photographs yourself, but the value of the criticism does not depend here, any more than it does in any other kind of critical work, on the critic's own practical ability. Often, in fact, objectiveness in making judgments suffers when the critic is a professional rival of the criticized artist.

Nature sets limits to the amount of influence the landscape photographer or the press photographer can have on the subject to be photographed. But the photographer working for advertising can exercise a more powerful influence on his subjects. By leaving out all incidentals and non-essentials he can achieve a thoroughly striking effect. Alternatively he can allow all the factors available—light and shade, depth in space, accessories and environment—to have full play so that they operate with their maximum illustrative power to give a distinctive atmosphere to the subject and increase its appeal. The photographer must know from the start whether the future observer will feel inclined to give the picture his attention for a long or a short time. A film slide, for example, which remains visible for perhaps five seconds, must in that space of time be completely absorbed and understood by the viewer if it is to be capable of fulfilling its task. In the same way, some photographs can only be effective when not encumbered by irrelevant material, when designed like a poster.

The situation is somewhat different with the "story-telling" photograph intended to illustrate a condition or event. The eye of the observer passes slowly over the picture, lingers at certain points, wanders back again and follows a route along the internal guide-lines of the picture. This optical exploration is generally led to pursue a predetermined course so that nothing uncomprehended is left over at the journey's end. That is why it is pointless to try to press as much meaningful content as possible into a picture. The limits of understanding are admittedly always variable, but such limits should not be tested. American magazine advertisements for semi-luxuries, household goods, automobiles and interior decoration are often so overloaded that the atmosphere of the picture is impaired rather than strengthened. The layout man must always remember when selecting the final picture that the subject must be discernible and surveyable.

Because of its wealth of possibilities for representation, photography has become, like graphic art, a medium of artistic expression. Micro-photographs and X-ray photographs fix truths that are invisible to the naked eye. Their order and their rhythm communicate novel, optically unusual fields of experience with great potential advertising value. A light

Illus. 13—Correct cropping makes a photograph a picture—it emphasizes content and values. Non-essentials may be removed, but the cropping must not make the picture too narrow. The atmosphere of the illustration must remain unchanged. A horizontal scene must remain horizontal, and the central features must not be denuded of a frame of reference. The smaller the final picture, the more emphatic (but the more sombre and less interesting, too!) is this seaport scene from Dalmatia.

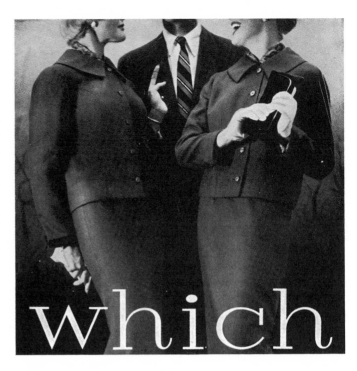

Illus. 14—A tastelessly cropped subject—with heads cut off! The keynote is the man's tie, but the postures and gestures of the three people, which could and should be important, are merely hinted at, while non-essential elements are given exaggerated weight. For both aesthetic and advertising reasons one can certainly now and then make use of the unusual, but even the out-of-the-ordinary must make sense.

source in random motion, oscillating in a dark room opposite a camera, makes it possible to fix movements which are beyond the limits of what can be shown in a drawing: they are reminiscent of the curlicues on paper money. Such varied effects can be created by photographic negatives and positives, by pictures surprinted on one another, by insertion of screens in photo-printing, by oscillating illumination and by changes in the quality of paper used, that it is no longer possible to recognize the finished product with any certainty as a photographic creation.

"Photo-montage" originated, as its name indicates, in the building up of subjects to create a new, pictorial unity. The intention is to create effects otherwise unattainable in photographs. Generally, photo-montages use parts of actual photographs, landscapes or people, in a new, often surrealistic context. Tourism uses this medium primarily to assemble into a single picture objects which cannot normally be photographed at the same time. However, photo-montages are only effective when illumination, perspective and the treatment of light and shade are not too violently in conflict with each other, and when the whole is not crammed and overloaded. Photo-

montages, when immediately recognizable as such, also have the disadvantage of undermining the observer's faith in the truth and objectivity of photography. Because of the apparent ease with which it can achieve fast and surprising effects with simple means, photo-montage has forfeited a great deal. It demands not only photographs, scissors and paste, but also creative ability and first-class pictorial matter harmonizing in all its tones and values.

"Photograms" are pictures made without a camera, by means of light and photo-sensitive paper alone. The paper is partly covered by sharply outlined organic or inorganic patterns; it is then illuminated and the object moved after a partial illumination; then illuminated again, and so on. The results are charming overlapping applications in many shades of grey, which a skilled operator can keep completely under control. Used in combination with other techniques for copying and enlarging, the method has possibilities for ever-new and interesting effects.

Also on the borders of photography is "nature printing," which can be carried out either by means of a photogram or by ordinary printing. Flat objects—leaves, threads, paper, etc.—are colored with printing ink and then pressed directly on to paper or a lithographic stone from which, after etching, prints can be made on paper. The Japanese, whose seas swarm with curious and fantastic fishes, even color these and make impressions of them on rice paper.

Drawing and photography meet in "glass engraving." A sheet of glass is coated with an opaque layer on which a drawing is made with a sharp needle. The finished plate is then copied like a negative on photographic paper.

This short survey, which is by no means exhaustive, since new means of expression are constantly appearing, outlines a field of representation in both the realistic and the abstract spheres which is very inadequately used in advertising.

CROPPING

What is true of photography in black and white applies equally to color photography. In both, cropping is all-important. It can eliminate those parts of the subject which are detrimental to the essential elements. It can moderate the garishness typical of many color photographs; colorfulness and gaudiness are not one and the same thing. If the object to be

photographed can be influenced by the photographer, it is easy for him to obtain harmonious color-schemes; it is more difficult where landscapes, topical pictures and portraits are concerned.

As in drawings, paintings and abstracts, the creative artist must bear in mind—in his capacity as intermediary between his client and the public—that the reader does not look at a photograph or drawing with the same eyes nor with the same expectations as its creator does. The observer accepts what is offered to him as unchangeable, though this does not of course mean that he is forbidden to criticize it.

The problems and technical difficulties which had to be overcome before or during the picture taking must not be apparent in the finished work lest the onlooker be distracted from the picture's message—which is to guide him and persuade him.

The effect of a picture, and accordingly its success as an advertisement, depends to a great extent on the lines of optical guidance in the picture and the way it is cropped.

The copy first made from a negative is the layout man's raw material. It is often not a usable picture until it has been cropped and until any necessary retouching has been done.

Illus. 15—Cropping has made the eye-guidance excellent. The intimate character of the event is underlined on either side by the striking impact of the whites and darks of the uniforms. Everything is concentrated on the hand with the pen. The distribution of color is as good as in a fine poster. If eye-guidance and movement do not aim at the focal point, it makes the whole picture ineffective.

Illus. 16—Many advertising photographs give the effect of snapshots, though they are the result of detailed planning and preparation. This scene was planned down to its smallest details, properly lit and the cropping decided on. The accent is on its most important part, the bar; the out-of-focus figures give the picture its atmosphere. A tight crop is permissible in this case, for the "head-cutting" is mitigated by their sketchiness.

It is important to preserve and bring out the atmosphere, the personal, special and unique elements in a picture, for we are always unconsciously influenced by romantic notions which affect our attitudes of approval or dislike. If you feel uncertain about a photograph, in deciding how to crop it, study the pictures and drawings of old and new masters. Rembrandt's drawings and paintings in particular are marvellously self-contained: there is not an inch too much or too little. Nothing can be taken away or added to them without endangering their equilibrium and rhythm. Any photographer or layout man who keeps an attentive eye on the works of the great painters will be capable of making or using pictorially good photographs.

There are open or closed, left-hand, right-hand, indifferent, static, dynamic, practical, emotional, truthful and lying photographs (even when they have not been touched up or otherwise falsified). By proper cropping, a photograph can be made to convey the diametrical opposite of its original message.

Because of the direction followed by the eye in reading, a left profile looks as if it were turned towards us, while a head looking towards the right seems to be turning away from the viewer. A runner starting on the left of a picture runs "into" it, while a starter from the right seems to be backing out of the picture. A landscape with a foreground subject on the left therefore seems to be running towards the right into the distance, and is called "open,"

The invisible cosmetic
that brings out the beauty in you
Perfume by Dana

What every beautiful woman knows, by heart! A perfume by Dana is the invisible cosmetic that comes in a bottle but is applied to the soul, creating beauty from inside out. Don't leave home without it. Truly well-dressed women never do.

DANA PERFUMES, FOR EVERY FACET OF BEAUTY / 20 CARATS, THE ESSENCE OF ELEGANCE

Illus. 17—The girl's eye exerts a hypnotic attraction on the reader, whose glance passes down the silhouette to take in the flask and the name before reading the text. The picture, rendered impersonal by its narrow crop, encourages the interested reader to agree with the advertiser's claims. His attention is aroused, and so is his inclination to buy.

while the same picture held against the light ("flopped" left to right) represents a closed or self-contained scene.

A picture cropped too small lacks air. Portraits cut too narrow seem stifled. The space in front of the face in profile portraits must be large enough. This applies equally to photographs of moving subjects. A jumping horse must be free at all points, but above all it must have room enough over its head, in front and below its hooves. Otherwise it will look as if it had been stuffed into a box.

A pole-vaulter needs to have the ground beneath his feet in the picture, as otherwise his performance cannot properly be appreciated. Mountain landscapes without a man or familiar-sized object in sight are pointless, for they offer no yardstick of comparison—unless the picture is intended to express omnipotence or awe-inspiring majesty symbolically.

If a head is shown only in a narrow section, cropping will enforce concentration on essentials, but it should never be overpowering or appear inorganic.

Irrelevant details which cannot be taken away by cropping should be removed by retouching.

Photographs of people often suffer because the space surrounding the chief figure is cropped in such a way that the picture is rimmed by bisected heads, halved arms, sliced-off non-essentials and parts of subjects which may or may not be interesting, as far as the viewer can judge.

Care should be taken to see that proper provision has been made for all photographs in the layout sketch from which the photographer must work. This of course assumes that the layout man himself has some knowledge of photography

If photographs must be made before the layout for a certain assignment, the photographer should work in conformity with the principles mentioned.

It is a mistake to ask an artist for an imitation

Illus. 19—Three hundred years ago an Italian artist, Archimboldo, painted human figures composed of fruits, flowers and vegetables. A forerunner of surrealism, he has had some clever successors among modern photographers. In certain places, these pictures can be quite effective, because the unusual, especially when it is offered with a witty touch, never fails to hit the mark.

Illus. 20—(Left) This illustrates a mistake made repeatedly in advertisements and tourist literature: Subjects of varying kinds, with no clearly visible lines of separation between them are shown from different angles, piled on top of each other. Foreground pictures, particularly when looked at from above, have their proper place below, nearest the onlooker. In any sequence from bottom to top, the middle-distance subjects should come next and finally the pictures showing distant views and sky. If the pictures have totally varied contents, they should not be assembled strip-fashion.

Illus. 21—(Right) A narrow shape may be justified: It makes some delightful solutions possible. In this case, however, violence has been done to the photograph by squeezing it into a pre-determined size. A mother looking at such an advertisement is likely to identify her own child with the unfortunate "squashed" baby and to react with distaste. The advertisement would fail in its purpose.

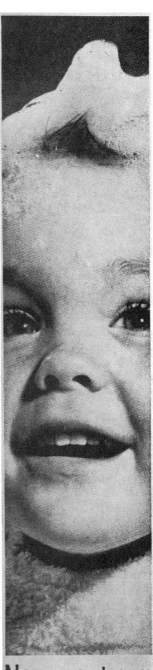

No more tears
from soap in the eyes

35

Illus. 22—This series of pictures is just right. The heads are equal in size, the crops appropriate. The first picture is a "left-hand" one, the others "right-hand" ones, so that the series, no matter where it appears on a page, gives the impression of a self-contained unity.

of a photograph. His work has qualities which no photograph can ever have. To bring them out and display them to their best advantage is the task of the layout man. If you use paintings and drawings by artists now dead, do so with reverence and make sure also that you can get the right to reproduce them. If the assignment requires it, you can of course also use portions of pictures, such as hands, a flower or some other element, but care should be taken not to "squeeze" a painting into another format or to trim its edges.

Illus. 23—A series of pictures from an American travel agency folder. The white lines separating the pictures are almost invisible. The two scenes on the left are seen as a unity, because of the pictorial sweep, and because the observer's standpoint and the landscape are similar. The newly created "mountain" in the middle, between the first and second pictures, is an irritating element, and the slope on the right of the middle picture leans against the tall building in the next picture. The building at the right in the third picture is badly cropped and we get no information about its size.

GRAPHIC ART AND PAINTING

A great artist once said that drawing means *leaving out*, and this is an essential truth about advertising art too. The purpose of an advertisement determines the way the object is to be represented pictorially. A poster must never be a "picturette." A diagrammatic drawing, on the other hand, must be able to supply satisfactory answers to all the questions likely to be asked. Non-essentials should appear in a picture only when they are necessary for the creation of a certain atmosphere. Art is often called upon to replace photography if a *photographic* effect is required. In industry, for instance, there are objects that are difficult to picture completely; they cannot be photographed satisfactorily because of their large size or the way they have been constructed. Following photographs or technical drawings of parts, therefore, photograph-like illustrations with "realism" can then be made for use in catalogues.

Illus. 25—With charcoals and pastels, vividly contrasting subjects as well as artistically delicate ones can be presented. Velvety three-dimensional tones, gracefully flowing lines and varied inner shadings yield effects which advertising can use. Pastel drawings made on rough paper can also be reproduced by newspaper screens, sometimes even as line engravings. Not only the concrete, however, but also the ideal, ornamental and abstract can be well represented by means of charcoal, chalk and pastel. Line drawings with these materials give a more "improvised" effect than India ink drawings.

Illus. 24—The poor quality of newsprint need not limit you to coarse-screen halftones for pictures. Effective as photographic portraits are fine-line pen drawings or scratchboard drawings, which bring out the essentials even better and also bridge the gap between poster effectiveness and realistic illustrative reproduction.

Illus. 26—(Left) Large-area projects for posters and other intensely colored printed matter for advertising purposes are created predominantly with tempera and other opaque colors. Intermediate tones are achieved here by mixtures and by lightening with white.

Illus. 27—(Right) Water-color painting uses transparent colors. Line and surface make an immediate appeal and seem more improvised than tempera work. A translucent paper base enhances the brilliance of the colors and halftones.

A photograph is just as incapable of replacing a good fashion-drawing or the incisive picture of a car. The photograph shows the object from a single viewpoint, but the beholder of a car co-ordinates so many individual impressions in a momentary glance or in fantasy that quite a

Illus. 28—Knowledge of the most commonly used artistic techniques and their application is important for the layout man. Pencil drawings win the attention of the reader by their tenderness and delicacy and the many tones of grey available to them. Photogravure, offset halftones and fine-screened letterpress halftones reproduce pencil drawings best. (Drawing by Werner Bürger.)

38

Illus. 29—Picture motifs with a poster effect can also be cut from colored paper. Not only posters, but also book jackets, packages and other advertising planned for long-distance effect can use this technique. The powerful simplification brought about by renouncing halftones and technical processes makes pictures easily recognizable by children too. (Illustration by Busso Malchow from a book for children.)

different picture of the car is bound to be produced by the one-eyed or "one-view" camera.

Fashion-drawings, too, exaggerate and omit. They must bypass vision to make a direct appeal to the feelings, while the photograph mercilessly presents to the eye all the small flaws and shortcomings that are impossible to eliminate entirely. Drawings appeal to the imagination; photographs convey facts. The consequence is that graphic artists have been

Illus. 30—A drawing broadly executed on scratch-board or scraperboard—a hard white cardboard coated with India ink. The finer lines are then scratched with needles and gravers into the white. The result, reminiscent of a woodcut, is most suitable for realistic representations to be reproduced as line cuts. (From an English magazine.)

Illus. 31—The character of a picture changes when it is flopped left to right. The eye probes each theme as if it were a written text, and accepts it either as an open or closed picture, according to whether the right edge is light or dark. In the left-hand picture, the eye peers into the distance, while in the right-hand one it finds nearness, intimacy, even something of constraint or confinement. The left-hand picture belongs properly to the left side of a layout; the right-hand one to the right side if justice is to be done to each version. (From an etching by Rembrandt; the original is on the right.)

employed in advertising fields where it might have been expected that the photographer would have had scope for his talents. Graphic artists with a gift for naturalistic representation are often hired for reasons dictated by printing techniques. The advertising appeal of a drawing, with its controlled manner of representation, is greater for women than men. Men

Illus. 32—India ink drawings executed with pen and brush are effective both as to line and surface. To loosen up large black areas, to let in light-colored compositions or to make corrections, opaque white tempera is used. The sharp contrast of black and white is most effective in newspapers: It makes the India ink drawing the most suitable medium for reproduction in newspapers and any publication printed by letterpress.

40

Illus. 33—Women like realistic representations of goods offered to them, at least where everyday things are concerned. But in this sphere, once reserved for the photographers, graphic art continues to gain ground. If artwork is naturalistically executed, it can eliminate non-essentials more effectively than a photograph, and lead the eye direct to essentials. The above picture puts the dew-fresh tomatoes alongside the steaming soup. The advertisement below combines abstract art with representation.

neutralize it by means of the ever-changing ways of representation it has at its disposal.

What has been said of drawing as an advertising medium is equally true of painting. Its real possibilities are just beginning to be utilized, as the purposes and intentions of creative painting on the one hand, and advertising on the other, and the views of those generally prefer to be guided by cold facts and plain speaking without any superfluous ornamentation.

So, advertising makes increasing use of graphic art to sell the objects of everyday life—foods and semi-luxuries, health and beauty culture, textiles, clothing, travel. Graphic art in the hands of really talented artists offers a wider range and far greater possibilities of capturing the public eye, than the flood of photographs which now deliver the world to our doorsteps—not to mention films and television. We grow accustomed to photography, and thereby have a lowering of the threshold for the reception of impressions. Graphic art, however, can avoid this danger or

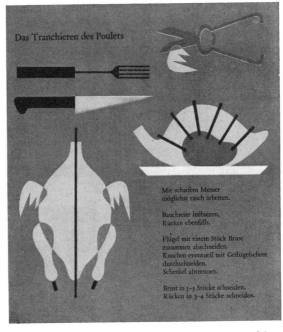

engaged in the two divisions, until recently seldom coincided.

While we are on the subject of words and pictures, let us try to define the distinctive features of *trash*. Trash is of course abundant in all fields of creative work. The difference between the trash and the genuine is like that between saccharine and cane sugar, the substitute and the natural substance. Trash is tasteless; but it is dangerous, too, because it often lurks behind good technical performance and tries to make an impression on our unconscious with false romanticism. Trash leaves the mind no time to react negatively. We are conquered more easily by vocal and musical trash than by the pictorial variety, for the ears accept the former more uncritically than the eyes do the latter. Seen or read, trash is obvious and escapable if the viewer has sensibility. A badly done piece of work need not of course be trashy: it becomes so only when it is pretentious, presumptuous, overloaded, snobbish. Trash flourishes in both plastic and graphic art, as well as in pictorial advertising. Sometimes it pretends to be modern or abstract, because even the educated person's ability to dis-

Illus. 34—To achieve patterns and halftone-like effects in line drawings, artists use self-adhering screened papers and transparent screen films, and insert them in India ink drawings. (From a Dutch catalogue.)

tinguish between good and bad in this kind of art assumes a certain sureness in making judgments. Trash of this kind is impudent, while naturalistic trash, which is directed mainly towards the masses with their undeveloped capacity for discernment, is generally sentimental. Superficial, erotically superheated, exaggeratedly drawn or photographed subjects with words and pictures evoking unfulfillable and therefore often suppressed wish-dreams have a special appeal. Trash is often found in advertising for this reason.

Illus. 35—Xylographs, wood engravings and woodcuts have retained their place as an illustration technique, especially in books, despite modern methods of drawing, reproduction and printing. (Wood engraving by Carl Tesche.)

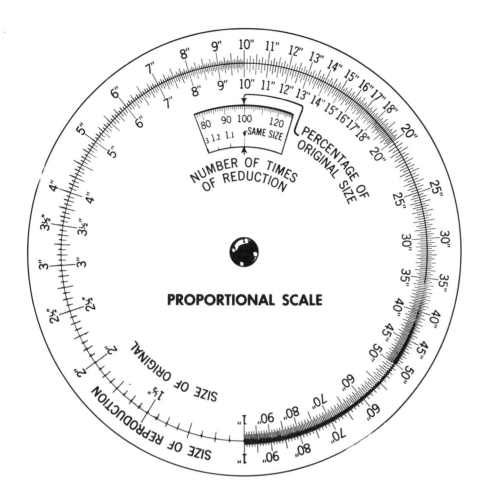

PROPORTIONAL SCALE

Illus. 36—Circular proportional slide rule for obtaining enlarged or reduced proportions of photographs and artwork.

SIZING THE PICTURE

There are two ways of fitting a photograph into a layout. If the space for the photograph in the layout has already been fixed, the photograph may have to be cropped to fit. If, however, the cropping can only be done one way, the size of the picture must be correspondingly enlarged or reduced.

To decide how the crop should be made, use four strips of black or white paper or two L-shaped pieces of cardboard, placed at right angles to each other, to cover the space that is not needed. The chosen area is indicated by short arrows or lines made with a grease pencil or with opaque white. The final size is often also noted on the back, or—when a light-table is used—also marked there. In any case, the crop marks, the final dimension in at least one direction, the position, instructions for the process photographer and for the retoucher should be given on the back of the photograph or on the front, if necessary, in grease pencil.

Illus. 37—(Below) Another way to scale a picture, larger or smaller, by use of a rectangle.

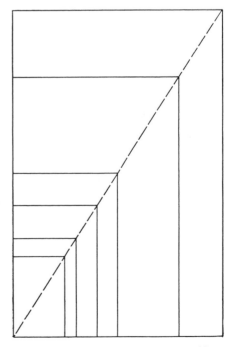

43

The simplest calculation of a size can be made by means of a diagonal. If you connect two opposite corners of a rectangle (photograph) by a diagonal, all the horizontal and vertical lines bounding the diagonal at any given point form rectangles of the same proportions.

For example: an original photograph 4 inches wide and 6 inches high (proportion $1:1\frac{1}{2}$) is to appear in a layout $2\frac{1}{4}$ inches high. Draw the diagonal. In the large rectangle draw a new line $2\frac{1}{4}$ inches high parallel to the tall side, so that it begins on the short side and ends right at the diagonal. If you draw a horizontal from this point, the new rectangle round the diagonal will be the size you want: $1\frac{1}{2}$ inches wide.

Even if the rectangle is the most commonly used shape for pictures, the possibilities of other shapes—circles and free forms—should be examined for advertising purposes. Bear in mind that pictures with lively subjects need a sedate outline, while restful contents—and also interesting contours in fashion photographs—can be effective without a natural background. For odd shapes, calculate for the final size in the same way, using points on the diagonal of a rectangle, and after that proceed with the outlining. If it is desirable to attain exact outlines immediately in the final size, use a pantograph. Better still, make an interim photograph (blueprint, sepia print or photostat) or an enlargement from the original negative in the desired size. If it is important to include the shading or solid areas of a picture in the layout, it is an advantage to work with photo proofs made in an enlarging camera or projector.

Particularly in the editorial departments of magazines, where snap judgments often have to be made on the effect of a title picture, vertical enlargers are commonly used. The original is projected from below on to a focussing screen. The picture appears as on a light-table. Adjust the distance. Lay a cut-out paper pattern on the image to show the best possible crop. When it has been decided, mark its essential outlines on a sheet of tracing paper. This will also serve as size information for the work of the processing photographer. The same method of finding the right crop is naturally also practicable for every other picture. It is the simplest way to fit illustrations into a previously determined frame. The work can of course also be done with an ordinary copying camera of the horizontal type, though tracing is then more difficult.

For the use of graphic artists, enlarging cameras are made that project pictures vertically on to a table, though the starting sizes these cameras will take are generally too small. For advertising purposes and the press, full-contrast glossy prints are desirable. Remember that each time a reproduction is made, the photograph loses some of its strength. In photographs of machines and many other similar objects, retouching is necessary. For work in color, photocopying is a simple matter with diapositives. If possible, avoid making copy photographs from halftone prints, as the screen of the first print will often leave undesirable moiré patterns when a new halftone is shot.

In making a halftone for letterpress printing, inform the engraver of the screen to be used. Screens vary between 65 lines per inch (for newspapers) to 133 or even 150 lines (on the best coated or art paper). No such instructions are necessary for line drawings from which line etchings are to be made. To decide on the density of the screen, first select the paper to be used for the printing. (See page 117 for more information on screens.)

Pictorial representation is going from strength to strength: the *observer* is beginning to overtake the *reader* in this restless age. The growth of picture newspapers, picture books, comics, television and color films is a sign which we hail with joyful anticipation or bewail, according to our disposition. Every creative worker, and so every creative designer in advertising, must take this growth into account if he does not want to be left out in the cold. The demands made by one of the two forms, however, must never be allowed to lead to neglect of the other. Words and pictures always make their most powerful impact when they form a well-balanced unit.

Illus. 38—Every picture, whether a painting, drawing or photograph, has its own inherent dynamism, which decides its usefulness. To be able to gauge the effectiveness of any picture, we must analyze it and find the thread with which its various parts are held together. In this pastel, a Swiss travel poster by Alois Carigiet, the foreground, middle distance and background are clearly separated, yet bound together by the well defined group of trees on the right. Despite the spacious background, the landscape thus appears self-contained. The cluster of houses and the coastline form a bowl which is reinforced by the parallel lines in the foreground. The verticals of the houses and the aqueduct lift the town out of its concealment up into the blue of the water and the sky, which is touched only by the tower of the cathedral. The lower third is held in place by the horses and the gate.

Color

In ADDITION to words and pictures, there is often a third functional element in advertising: color. Color can intensify both text and illustrations by endowing them with special characteristics, but it can also make its presence felt as a formative element in its own right. Contrary to the intellectual appeal of word and line, color primarily communicates emotional values, and these are indispensable in advertising.

Color dominates most of what happens to us and what we experience in our lives. It exerts a decisive influence not only on our eyes, but on all our other senses. Its psychological effect, combined with our subconscious awareness of age-old symbolism attached to it, makes color an important factor in any visual appeal addressed to human beings. Every individual's well-being and state of mind are dependent on the quantity of light he encounters.

Even if the effect of color harmonies in advertising work is more important than knowing the entire theory of color, it is nonetheless necessary to explain the basic elements of the latter.

SUNLIGHT AND THE SPECTRUM

Everything that surrounds us receives its color and form from the white light of the sun. As the intensity of sunlight decreases in the autumn and winter, and every evening too, all colors become duller and weaker, until finally only dim, dark shades of grey are visible.

Sunlight is white; but it is composed of radiations of varying wave-lengths. If a sunbeam is directed through a three-sided prism, its light is broken up into a colored band, the solar spectrum. Like the rainbow—which results from the refraction of the light in mist and raindrops—there is a color scale used by artists that ranges from red through orange, yellow, green and blue to indigo and violet.

The spectrum shows as visible light about 160 separately distinguishable shades, continuing beyond violet to the invisible ultra-violet rays and ending in the cosmic rays. This division of sunlight, normally only visible in a prism or the rainbow, is the cause of the colors we see in everything around us. This can be easily verified by noticing how the appearance of an object changes when it is subjected to radiation by artificial light of different colors. It either absorbs light-rays or reflects them.

If an object reflects all the rays that impinge on it, it looks white; if it absorbs all of them, it looks black. A body that absorbs all the groups of rays except green, which it reflects, looks green. What is colored and visible, therefore, is reflected light. The brightness of

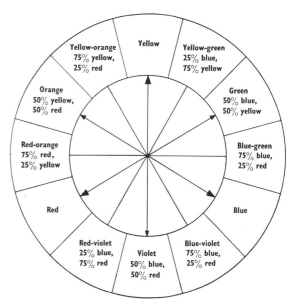

Illus. 39—The color wheel.

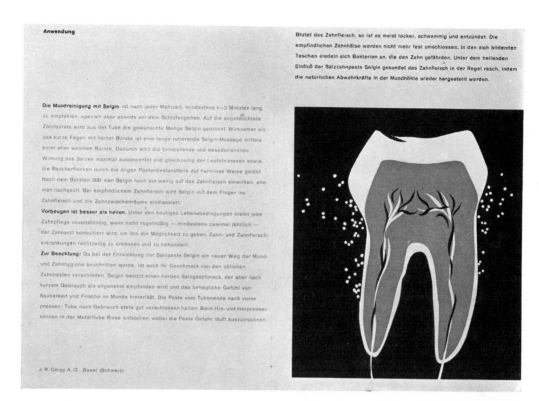

Illus. 40—Type is seldom included in the color scheme of an advertisement. But what a surprising contrast in weights is caused by the alternation of black and grey in this text! (Enzo Rösli, Switzerland.)

every color is determined by the intensity of reflection.

If reflection of the entire range of colors by an illuminated object is equally low over its whole surface, the visible result is a more or less bright grey.

All these colors, known as body colors, become visible only as a result of the light that falls on them. In contrast to them are the colors of light-rays themselves, which maintain their color even in a dark room. According to the same scientific laws by which white sunlight produces all the colors of the rainbow in the spectrum (with the exception of black, which is not a color, but the absence of color), the cones of radiation in all colors together concentrated on a point of a black surface reproduce white. This mixture of colors, called *additive*, is of merely theoretical importance in art. In everyday life, in advertising, and in the printing industry, it is only the *subtractive* mixture of colors that matters. Such a blend is so called because color values are covered, removed, taken away in each mixture. If all painting or printing colors are mixed (or overprinted) the final result will be black.

In a color wheel, the spectrum is in the form of a circle, with the three *primary colors,* red, yellow and blue, equidistant from one another. Theoretically, they contain no admixture of any other color; they are pure. Immediately opposite the primary colors in the circle are their *complementary colors,* each of which consists of a mixture of two of the primary colors. Opposite yellow is violet, composed of red and blue in equal halves. Facing red is green, consisting half of blue and half of yellow. Orange, composed of half yellow and half red, is the complementary color of blue.

Subdividing the color wheel can be continued: each hue has its complementary counterpart. However, the wheel lacks some shades which (in spite of their absence from the spectrum) are of considerable importance for us, for example, grey, pink and brown. These hues are not produced merely by mixing the

47

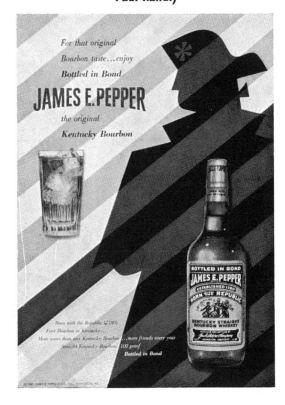

spectrum colors, but by lightening or darkening them with white, black or the mixed color formed from these, the neutral grey. Pink is red lightened with white; browns originate from orange or red mixed with black.

Colors are thus units whose position on the wheel has to be determined and defined. But the mutual relationships of colors, their harmonies and contrasts, are imponderable. Every association of one color with another is a creative process, the successful results of which depend on the insight of the artist and on many indefinable factors. Still, experience shows that we can confirm the recurrence of certain phenomena without being bound to raise them to the status of laws.

Complementary colors (opposite colors on the wheel) furnish the strongest contrasts. They provoke the eyes and when looked at over a long period become annoying. The situation is different when one of the two colors is dominant, and the second functions as a supplementary color. In this case the stronger, more persistent result is produced when the lighter color appears on a dark background. White or yellow text prints brighter on a black foundation, than does black text on a white or yellow ground. Each counter-color makes the other color appear more luminous in proportion to the amount of that color which it does not itself have. For instance, on a blue-violet ground, yellow-orange looks more intensely yellow than it is in reality.

Triads of colors can also be produced from the color wheel by trisection. Take a triangle joining the primary colors of the wheel, and rotate it to join other color-triads: for example, yellow-green, blue-violet and red-orange. Color triads are the primary colors or their first mixtures. Triads too are rich in contrasts and should therefore only be used cautiously, according to weight. Tetrads of opposite colors are formed by the application of a cross to the color wheel (one of these can be left out), but are usually too garish. The color of the paper will contribute to any color effect.

Adjacent colors in the color wheel can be visually separated from each other with difficulty and therefore have no separate visual value. Two colors close to each other, say violet and blue, need as a contrast and a counterweight the color opposite the middle of the two, in this case yellow-orange.

You will use the colors of the spectrum alone less frequently than you will use the tones formed by lightening and darkening them.

Lightenings and darkenings of a color are not effective for advertising purposes if they are used at the same time as the base color. Thus, for example, we find a combination of light brown, vermilion and pink an impossible color scheme. Graduated blue or yellow tones are less sensitive to the eye when used side by side.

If grey tones alone are employed in drawings near black and white, their mutual distances should be equal. A semi-circle showing all tones of grey between black and white in a continuous sequence has in the middle the *only* grey that is possible as a graduation to the base colors. With two tones of grey, the semi-circle must be trisected, and so on.

COLOR SYMBOLISM AND THE TRANSFORMATION OF COLOR

What is the attitude of people today towards color? Using a simple color symbolism, they are apt to think of red as the color of passion, to associate white with innocence and black with mourning. This does not tell us much. People call colors as warm or cold, active or passive. Red and orange are imagined as warm colors because they are linked with blood or fire. The blue side of the spectrum is thought to be cold. The reactions produced by green oscillate between these extremes, according to the predominance of yellow or blue.

Our attitudes to individual colors and color groups are collective and unconscious. They are a part of our culture and cannot be changed. The effect of cold and warm colors—at least as far as the primary colors and the mixed colors of the first grade are concerned—is the same among all people of the same race.

We are inclined to call a dark color "heavy" —we regard one color as weightier than another when it seems darker. A little orange in red makes it lighter, a touch of blue heavier.

Red is an aggressive, "foreground" color; it pushes itself forward and always takes the upper hand when used together with equally large areas of another color. Blue is different: it is the color of distance, perhaps because the sky appears blue. It does not gain weight until it darkens. Yellow and white reflect strongly and therefore seem "larger than life." There is a saying: White makes heavy, black slenderizes.

This collection and division of colors, and their identification with sensuous stimuli, with other symbols and contexts, have influenced the artistic creativeness of mankind since the dawn of history. Among primitives and in the ancient civilizations, in classical antiquity and later in Byzantium, in Italy of the Middle Ages (with such typical artists as Giotto), and in church painting, especially in the great Gothic cathedrals of France and Germany, color is employed more as a spiritual element than naturally and formatively.

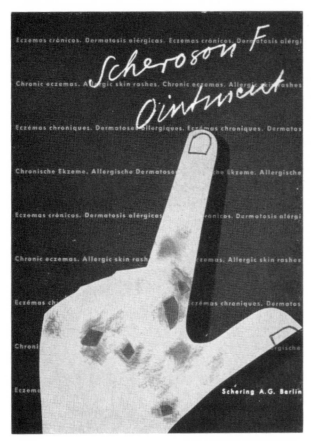

Illus. 43—A very striking page from a brochure. It is not only convincing in the way its pictorial elements have been built up: it yields additional effects through the use of advanced printing techniques. The first color, a dull red, is used only in the drawing of the hand and the lines of type in the background, while the shadow of the hand stands out in clear relief over the dull black background by the use of overprinting in a glossy red. The brand name is printed in white lacquer by the silk-screen process.

The Middle Ages identified a spiritual state with colors and color harmonies much more strongly than we do. Though we stand lost in wonderment before the polychromatic magnificence of Gothic stained-glass windows, we lack the audacity to produce anything comparable. Our thinking has become too rationalistic. The discovery that the ancient Greeks had gaily painted their white marble statuary was received with shock and mixed feelings by modern lovers of antiquity.

After the end of the Middle Ages, a general decrease of color intensity became noticeable. Preferences have developed for plain colors and simple compositions. In the Rococo period, colors became soft and delicate; all shades appeared to be blended, lightened with pastel-like shades. The Empire period showed strong contrasts once more, although they were limited to a small range of colors. Early Victorian tastes were in the direction of earthy colors. The early Twentieth century continued the process of decolorization. It seems almost as if delight in bright colors declines the more powerfully the achievements of civilization advance. Peoples living outside the equalizing influences of our civilization generally have more of a pronounced sense of color—a fact that can easily be confirmed by looking at examples of primitive and folk art from all parts of the world.

A wave of colorfulness followed the first World War, but its manifestations were so harsh and ungraduated, above all in architecture and interior decoration, that it did not succeed in permanently asserting itself at that time. In feminine things today, in fashions and homemaking, there are gratifying new color notes. More colorfulness in the home today is certainly due to the influence of women. In moderation we ought to be prepared to learn from this. Our drab workaday world has not yet really accepted color as something essential or fitting. It is still regarded as a mere supplement.

For a hundred years now, black-and-white photography has been affecting our capacity for appreciating color. In the monotone printing of picture newspapers and other illustrated publications, both red and green become grey. Only the different gradations of films and papers, filters and other methods of enrichment manage to keep the completely different natural colors apart in the scale of grey shades. Color photography has had the indisputable merit of restoring and re-promoting the capacity for seeing in color, even if colorfulness is occasionally confused with gaudiness. Films and the printing industry, the principal communicators of color, exert themselves to make the best possible use of it. It is to be hoped that in this way colorfulness will come into its own again.

It has been universally acknowledged that color (perhaps unconsciously) has a great

50

influence on our well-being. Color is becoming more and more important at work too. Machines are no longer painted in a monotonous dark grey: they are given practical colored coats to help their users find pleasure in their work and to add to their contentment. Machines are divided into color zones: different shades are used to give danger signals at special points. Decorative materials, walls and floors are becoming gayer and more colorful every year—a step forward that can only be welcomed!

It is a rewarding task for people engaged in advertising too, to create new elements of value and symbols of quality with the use of color. In today's advertising, we are still far too shy in using color, and hardly employ it at all as a constructive element by itself.

COLOR'S SIGNIFICANCE IN ADVERTISING

What is the significance of color in advertising? Color addresses itself to the emotions, and its mere presence can have a pacifying or exciting effect, chilling or warming, strong or tender. Appealing to the preferences of the spectator, it serves to represent abstract ideas such as peace, movement, danger, death. It makes a more immediate appeal to the eye than black and white. Moreover, color "sticks" more strongly to the conscious and unconscious mind than do line drawings or monochrome halftones. People are inclined to identify things in their surroundings with colors rather than with shapes and words: concepts such as desert, sky, leaves, coffee, wine, for example, evoke chromatic picturizations. Color is more natural than colorless black, even if the color used in a picture is not the actual color of the prototype. The fact that the link between a color and a product, consistently pursued, leads to subconscious identification, is used by advertising artists with particular success in the creation of an image for a commodity.

Aside from the general, collective attitudes to certain colors (white identified with innocence, red with love, blue with loyalty, black with grief, etc.) which we have already mentioned, everyone of course has his own personal likes and dislikes. People prefer certain colors

and react to certain color harmonies. However, these tastes do not stay unchanged throughout a person's life; they alter as we grow older. The fondness of children for red and strong colors changes as they grow up and gain an increased capacity for distinguishing between shades. And this evolution of taste does not follow the same course in men as it does in women.

Preferred colors and color harmonies are generally chosen subconsciously, and the impulses that give birth to them are quite mysterious. Like the longing for beauty and clothes, the imitative urge can be decisive. To be in the fashion swim one year, you may choose violet, the next year brown will be all the rage, until it turns out that prominent people are wearing blue. So it goes—colors have vogue, and the advertising artist has to keep in step, or one step ahead.

A brilliant sunny environment usually encourages a preference for powerful color compositions, as in Italy, Hawaii, and in most sub-tropical countries. Delicate shades are felt to be more attractive in cooler areas where the blue of the sky is paler (for example in England and Scandinavia). Civilized peoples love mediate colors; country folk keep their inborn, naïve fondness for strong colors, while city dwellers prefer blue, grey and mixtures. So, just as colors are identified with moods, they are also related to conceptions of taste and physical conditions.

Red is the color of fire, revolution, sensuality, desire. It is a youthful color, and so it is popular with children, and with unsophisticated primitive races. As it is a forceful color, drowning all others, it is not suitable for bases or backgrounds unless on the dark side—crimson and maroon. A blue point on a red surface produces the effect of a hole, while a red point seems to sway over a blue ground. A red point on black seems to shine as brightly as one on a white ground. Red is a preferred color on posters, but it is less frequently to be found as a covering on packages: it has too much life of its own, is too self-assertive, and so cannot subordinate itself to the goods it encloses. Used in drawing, on the other hand, red is striking on both light and dark back-

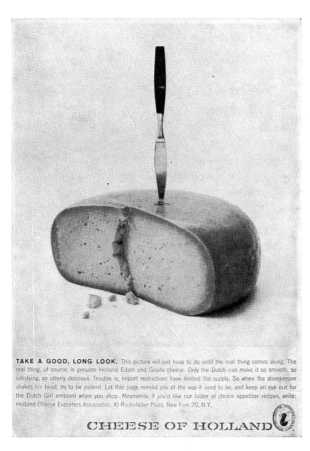

TAKE A GOOD, LONG LOOK. This picture will just have to do until the real thing comes along. The real thing, of course, is genuine Holland Edam and Gouda cheese. Only the Dutch can make it so smooth, so satisfying, so utterly delicious. Trouble is, import restrictions have limited the supply. So when the storekeeper shakes his head, try to be patient. Let this page remind you of the way it used to be, and keep an eye out for the Dutch Girl emblem when you shop. Meanwhile, if you'd like our folder of choice appetizer recipes, write: Holland Cheese Exporters Association, IO Rockefeller Plaza, New York 20, N.Y.

CHEESE OF HOLLAND

Illus. 44—A cheese with an exclamation mark: the color of the advertisement is limited to the vivid yellow of the rind and the more delicate tint of the cheese itself. The black handle of the knife and the neutral grey of its blade thereby have a more direct effect: they attract the eye and lead it downwards. The knife is like a call, an incisive statement. The stencil-type capital letters subtly call attention to the fact that the product is imported, awakening associations with distant countries, seaborne freight, ships with exotic names.

grounds. It is an inflammatory color: if you want to sell cool, refreshing goods, never offer them garbed in red! Like all gleaming colors—among others, white, yellow and orange—red has enlarging properties, especially when contrasts reinforce its illuminating power. A yellow package, sparingly provided with dark lettering, looks larger than a dark package with yellow text.

Red, like all warm colors, appeals to the surface senses, while the colder blue, blue-green and their compounds associate themselves with deeper feelings.

All shades of yellow, green and violet are indifferent in value, depending on the colors associated with them; they can be either positive and active in effect, sensuous and intellectual, or negative and passive.

In pink—red diluted with white—red loses all its strength and expresses sweetness, tenderness, poetry.

If red and yellow are darkened, the result is a large and important group of browns, ranging from ochre to copper. There is no

common denominator for brown. All the colors in this group, however, have certain qualities in common: earthiness, solidity, firmness, matter-of-factness. Advertising makes use of brown as a basic appeal to housewives and to give an impression of warmth.

Next to red, yellow has the greatest illuminating power, but it is more ethereal and cannot be so precisely defined. It has a cool effect compared with the incandescent yellow-orange, but is warmer than yellow-green. It thus has many faces, and appeals more to the intellect than to the heart. Its character becomes recognizable only through the presence of a second color. When it tends towards green, it becomes more substantial and tangible.

Green is the organic color *par excellence:* it is close to nature and calms the nerves; it is well modulated, neither cooling nor heating. If it tends towards blue, it becomes watery. Blue-green—and turquoise, which is derived from it—rightly symbolize water and flowing motion in general. Blue-green is the opposite of fire.

Blue is passive, dreamy, isolating, even when it is brightened by the addition of white. It gives us the impression of being a clean, pure color, and is therefore used wherever hygienic associations with products are to be evoked.

Violet suggests introspection, meditation, mystery, the occult and exotic. Even when mixed with white to form lilac or mauve, it keeps the spectator at a distance. Purple, verging more on blue, is more worldly than violet, but remains aristocratic and dignified.

Gold, located in the vicinity of orange, is regarded as a warm color and is used accordingly, while silver is cold and akin to the neutral grey. Silver is difficult, needing supplementation by a warm shade if it is to have a positive effect. Tinplate cans therefore need warmly colored labels.

The long scale of greys between black and white (in monotone diapositives about thirty shades can be distinguished) is familiar to us through photographs, films, newspapers and books. We seldom take the trouble to "translate" monotone pictures back into colors: grey has become self-sufficient. Advertising, however, renounces this achromatic color if variegated hues are available. A neutral silver-grey shade may have a restrained, unobtrusive action, but it is of no service at all as far as most advertising material is concerned.

Black is the achromatic "color" of darkness, nothingness. In its advertising aspects, nonetheless, it has a positive quality, for it awards all colors of the spectrum when placed on it, an enhanced illuminating power, while it makes pastel shades still paler.

White is neither cold nor warm. Except for yellow—which is close to white in brightness—and pale shades mixed with white, all colors on a white ground are effective.

There are no such things as noxious, repulsive or "cheap" colors. Such opinions are based invariably on compositions of colors and color schemes, which are inappropriate to their subject and apportion emphasis wrongly.

What is important is not only the qualitative, but also the quantitative assembling of colors. A red text or drawing on a white ground produces quite a different effect from white text on red. In fact, it is almost possible to speak of an *active* inversion, such as in a photographic negative. Yellow lettering on a black ground is more legible than black on yellow, or white text on black, where only single words are concerned. The eye obtains more forceful light impulses, but it tires more rapidly. The more intense a color is, therefore, the more economically it should be used in combination with other colors, especially when the viewer will be forced to tolerate it for a lengthy period of time. This explains the absence of many popular colors in furniture, wallpapers and carpets.

On a red ground, only an equally powerful color will hold its own in the form of a drawing. Shades such as pink, grey and brown are drowned in red, and only black and white can assert themselves, or—if the drawing is a really strong one—yellows and blues too. On the less energetic yellow, because of the light ground, a wide range of colors is suitable for drawing, more than is possible on blue. A two-colored foundation can be thoroughly attractive, though it has become evident that a clear order of rank in the succession of colors generally has a better effect.

The pulling power of much advertising is dependent to an increasingly powerful degree on colorfulness. It is primarily the colorfulness of a package that makes it appeal to the potential buyer—not merely the intensity of the color, but its harmonious composition. It is not at all immaterial whether a package is provided with equally wide red and yellow stripes, or with narrow red stripes on a yellow ground, or with yellow stripes on red. A package with red lettering on a yellow base leads a buyer to make quite different assumptions from those which a red package with yellow text evokes.

Colors and color harmonies have been tested and the results obtained evaluated for advertising purposes. The conclusions arrived at can never of course have more than a relative value, and that only for a limited category of people, because preferences vary according to age, nationality, even locality and social status. They can therefore be fitted only approximately into a general plan. We can never be sure, either, whether the results of our research will still be valid ten years from now. Like advertising itself, color values are perpetually in a state of flux. Appraisals made by means of tests and for psychological reasons can never be anything but supports, to be used occasionally and carefully. They can never be rules, for they are based on day-to-day experience, not on immutable laws of nature.

EVERY WELL-CONSTRUCTED piece of work, and so every advertisement, is an arrangement of harmonies and contrasts. Whether in epic proportions or concentrated form—in any case, according to the function to be served—the object represented is intended to be seen, noticed and remembered. Just as a picture or a word can change its meaning when disturbed or lifted out of context, so every element of a layout must be immovable and irreplaceable and be so clear that any alteration made to it will be to its disadvantage. Advertising is an appeal and a challenge, but at the same time an unceasing battle waged against monotony and indifference. If it is to be effective, it must therefore make use of every means available to vanquish the humdrum pace of everyday life and habit. It calls to its aid all the possibilities of tension and conflict inherent in words and pictures and in the contrast of these two.

There are infinite varieties of ways and ever-new means of building up the pictorial and textual elements of an advertisement so that its success will be assured. The starting point, however, is always the same. The plan of the advertisement is a layout of creative work in both words and pictures; the interplay of the two in the layout is what decides the quality of an advertising appeal.

The great variety of good and effective advertising techniques available to business proves that there is no standard pattern for a good layout. In creative work there is no formula and there are no infallible recipes. "Everything flows," that age-old saying, is vitally true in the advertising world. Advertising is always rich in new, unsuspected directions of activity. One man may prefer to work in strict accordance with tradition; aiming at distinction, he disdains out-of-the-way effects and works statically. Another looks for what is unused and strives to achieve a dynamically sound appeal. The picture as an eye-catcher is the preferred medium of some, the telling phrase alone that of others. It is important however to bear in mind, when attempting to solve every advertising problem, the category of people to whom the plan is being addressed,

The Technique of Layout

and to ask yourself whether the envisaged effect will be attained, whether the appeal will hit its target. A beautiful design can be completely sterile if the job the advertisement has to do was not well thought out. On the other hand, this principle should not be carried to the opposite extreme—paying no attention at all to aesthetic considerations—for the people approached by the advertisement are never without standards or feelings for real values. Every good layout, therefore, should not only be effective as an advertisement as far as form is concerned; it should also be enriched with beauty, always a positive asset.

The layout must adapt itself to our reading habits if it is to be successful. We start reading every page at the top and from the left, and we do the same unconsciously when we look at pictures. Layouts must take into account this "reading rhythm."

It is also important to know how the layout is to function. What kind of products are to be sold? Where? When? In what environment? Readers of magazines usually have more time to spare than newspaper readers, and readers of catalogues more time than readers of folders. There are many tasks to be fulfilled, many demands to be considered. The only firm and unalterable standards are the functions and effects of size, line, surface, color and space, at rest and interchanged.

Keep in mind always that layout has two

components: text and picture. Text is the backbone of all visual advertising, while the picture intensifies and explains or operates as an eye-catcher.

In layout drawing, there is nothing better than constant sketching. All printed advertising material needs originality. Look for the new, the different. Study of others' advertising trains the eye, but an analysis of other people's material should never tempt one to imitate. The good examples reproduced here from all over the world are intended to act only as incitements to the reader's own creative powers. Each of them is just one solution of a layout problem out of a countless number of possible ones. No layout is *the* solution; it is simply *a* solution. The same assignment will be interpreted and carried out by the next man in quite a different way, and yet both may be right. Everyone follows his own path, so the only function of this book can be to show a *possible* way, not to give final solutions.

UNITY AND CONTRAST

To overcome indifference, verbal tension is not the only thing necessary in building up printed matter; pictorial excitement is needed too. An advertisement becomes fascinating through contrasts, and thus raises itself above the ranks of its competitors. But the contrast need not always be within the advertisement itself. If a printed advertisement is surrounded by other advertisements on which it can have no influence, a restrained notice enclosed by or placed between violently agitated rivals may prove striking precisely because of its calm. It follows that similar and equivalent things placed side by side forfeit their effectiveness. When we design advertisements, packages or posters, we are generally not aware of the advertising work our prospective competitors for attention are doing, so the unusual, the surprising, is always a positive asset. Merely copying what has been successful (even your own work) injures the copier most, for freshness and originality are among the most important prerequisites for a forceful appeal.

Copy should be as brief as possible, and it should be readably arranged so that it can be vividly assembled and made up. The layout man's most heartfelt desire is for copy that is interesting both in its visual form and in live action. The copywriter should therefore divide his text up systematically into sections according to the ideas and points of view it contains, so that the layout man can easily visualize it. The picture—photograph, drawing or decoration—is the counterpart of the copy and can either overrule or be subordinate to the copy, but must never have the same optical weight. Clarity must always prevail over all considerations. Without clarity, text and picture will destroy each other's effectiveness: with it, the contrast between copy and picture can contribute towards the ultimate impact of an advertisement. The question of when the picture shall dominate and when the copy shall have the upper hand depends on many considerations and cannot be answered in a general way. It is important, however, in every case that both elements compose a synthesis, so that they cannot be separated from each other without injuring the effect of the whole.

Unity and contrast are important for giving appropriate visual form to the intentions of an advertisement. Repose and harmony have lost a great deal of their charm in the highly strung conditions of the present age; tension is drawn tightly, to hardly bearable extremes of excitement. Graphic advertising is always on the lookout for novelty, unsuspected chords, the piquant and individualistic, surprising and occasionally even glaring, exotic and discordant colors, lines and surfaces—all without arousing discomfort either in copy or in illustration. Balanced form and quietness, the traditional and the conservative, have retained their old positions only in one small area of visual communication: in scholarly papers, in ceremonial announcements, testimonials, and of course also in high-class book publishing. The modern way, with asymmetrical composition, has not succeeded in making its way into these fields.

Concepts such as restfulness, movement, uniformity and variety can be represented in drawing; they are understood everywhere in the same way. (See Illus. 45 on next page.)

The horizontal (1) gains effect through its stillness; it seems to symbolize repose. A

Illus. 45

regular, uniform rhythm of horizontal lines, either in illustration or in text, if long enough and clearly spaced, has a quieting effect. The vertical (2) strives upward; it symbolizes growth and life. The oblique line (3, 4) is unsteady, restless, seeming about to fall. It is the sign of movement. It needs a counterweight in the design, to intercept it or absorb its unrest.

The square (5), formed from the lines of repose and life, is self-contained. This, the most important of all the elementary patterns created by man, has a tranquillizing effect and is therefore dedicated to confining moving elements and thus make them endurable. The solid circle (6) is the natural form of self-contained calm, while the rotating circle (7)

56

represents the simplest form of continuous movement. Circles rotating in contrasting directions (8) cause restlessness. The same applies to the alternating movement of a single circle, as in the balance wheel of a clock. The division of an area into mere equal fields by halving and further subdivision is monotonous, often to the point of tedium (9, 10).

Just as a moving point becomes a line, so a surface arises from a straight line moving sideways, and a volume from a surface moved in another dimension. The juxtaposition, opposition and composition of points, lines and surfaces can produce both concordant and discordant notes. Just as the advertising appeal itself is a challenge to complacency, so every good advertisement, every appeal, depends on contrasts.

There are great varieties of contrasts, but they can all be reduced to a few basic forms. The first of them is the opposition of directions: two straight lines (11) running different ways. This elementary counter-movement is used again and again in advertising. A contrasting movement is also produced by the up-and-down of the zigzag (12) or the opposed movement of different curves (13) which need not even intersect each other. A fluently mobile line of lettering over straight text supplies the most practical example of such a contrast. Heaviness and lightness side by side are a contrast in weight (14), as for example in a single line placed opposite a photograph.

Contrasting forms (15) likewise have a forceful effect.

Contrasts of color and shade never fail to provide attractive solutions. Black and white (16) offer the most powerful opposition, but every color placed with another is capable of achieving fresh effects in harmony or contrast. Opposing colors do not have to be orgies of clashing hues; harmonies, even when obtained with surprising means, have a more pleasing effect than violent contrasts, which usually look cheap. Halftones achieved by means of screens (17) or other processes are very popular in printed advertising. As in drawings, varying values of grey can also be obtained in text by cleverly alternating thin and bold-face types, small and large fonts, set-solid and leaded-out matter. Using preprinted halftone papers makes the task of the layout man easier. Surface-contrasts result from placement of areas of different contents and weights (18, 19, 20) against each other.

This illustrates a point that can hardly be over-emphasized in layout work: blank areas have the same function and significance as printed ones. The white space is not simply what is left over; it is important as a counterpoise and contrast to the liveliness of the illustration and text matter. The white space is a building unit like the window is in architecture, an opening full of life. Every effort should be made in an assignment to consider not only the illustrated area but also the white

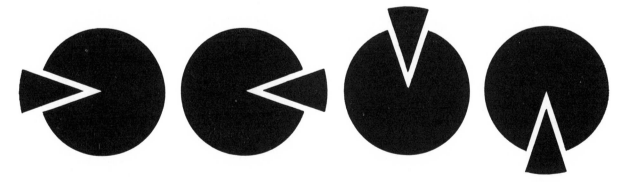

Illus. 46—Arrangements to guide the eye in a certain direction and to make reading follow a predetermined course are shown in these examples. The first wedge seems to be forcing itself into the cut, the second to be leaving the circle. The wedge above the circle seems about to fill the opening, while the fourth is dropping out. In building up a page, placing pictures and deciding how to crop pictures, it is important to know that compositions can be built up or torn apart in this way.

A   B   C   D

Illus. 47

space. Its appearance is just as decisive for the quality of the work as the printed surface.

Repose and liveliness are shown by the next two contrast sketches (21 and 22). A more penetrating opposition than that caused by a vertical and a horizontal is the combination of a straight line and an oblique one, though it tends to give a fidgety impression.

Reverses or inversions (23) are popular: lines of type that begin positively and continue in white on a picture with a dark background. A too-rapid change from negative to positive should be avoided. Harmony can be achieved by four-sided (24) and two-sided symmetry.

Effects of the most varied kinds can be obtained by tone-value contrasts. Illustration 47 shows four variations on a theme. The first drawing is reversed in the second. Though black and white are balanced in both A and B, the latter has the effect of a negative drawing, while A looks positive. White acts on the left, and black on the right, as the foundation on which the contrary color stands. B has the greater advertising value when used as a newspaper advertisement, for example. It then seems more strongly outlined against its companions. Naturally, violent contrasts of this kind are seldom used, for they do not make an attractive impression. Moreover, the simple transposition of intersected surfaces such as the point and the triangle in this case, is always hazardous as both parts seem restless. The third variant (C) renounces broad or crude effects: its various greys are well balanced. A wealth of grey tones is very effective in intaglio or gravure, which correctly reproduces artistic

values and photographs. Newspaper print generally fails to do justice to delicate shades, and makes them look either dull or excessively hard. The fourth variant (D) contains only two tonal stages, pure white and a grey in varied densities of line. In this example there is a lack of "dominants." These are often lacking in color printing too, if the color tones are indistinctly ranged in order of depth—if, for instance, the brightness-values of yellow, red, green and blue are equal. The juxtaposition of equally strong colors creates brightly colored, shrill advertisements in which colors "kill" each other.

LAYOUT AS A PLAN OF ACTION

The form and methods of illustration to be employed are determined by the task the layout has to perform. A layout is a ground-plan which should give everyone concerned a chance to contribute his share and do his best to bring the work to a successful conclusion. The competitive battle in modern business, however, has resulted in the word "layout" being applied to drafts or projects which are in fact finished drawings. The idea behind this practice, often employed by advertising agencies, is that the creative layout man, after the main outlines of the projected advertisement have been laid down for him, is in a position, thanks to his expert know-how, to plan word and picture in the best possible way. The client is therefore well advised to accept the work just as it is handed over to him. The finished layout, however, in this case, has to be the final outcome of many rough sketches.

58

There is no fixed pattern to predetermine the course of an advertising assignment. As a rule, it is the client whose wishes decide the sequence of events. Only rarely does the layout man initiate the whole procedure, or decide in his drawings where the separate elements are to be placed or what is going to be needed in the way of text and illustrations. Usually the text and headlines which layout and artwork must follow have been fixed in advance. Copywriters with a gift for pictorial expression make the artist's layout and planning work easier.

A satisfactory solution to a layout problem can only be produced if everyone concerned in the work understands just what the next man has to do, if it is clear to the layout specialist that layout is not a question of the indifferent putting-together of pictorial and verbal units: they must follow a clear and logical sequence. Striking effects can only be obtained by means of intelligently planned contrasts calculated to arouse the reader's interest visually.

Layout begins with thumbnail sketches, simple outline drawings in which an attempt is made to arrive at a smoothly flowing synthesis of copy and illustrations. Outlines are sketched out on the actual size of the paper to be used, and drawings are made with a few lines of picture, type and the other formative elements. A start is made with the most important elements, the largest ones. Just as we begin to plan the furnishing of a room with the biggest piece of furniture and finish with the smallest, so it is in a layout. Shapes and relative sizes and proportions must be correctly determined at the start; otherwise, during the later and more detailed work, the sources of error will turn up again and again to hamper the progress of the work and make realization of the sketched effect unattainable. We take the best elements from the first thumbnail sketches and work out something better from them. Any mistakes will be recognized and avoided in the new design.

Whether the other people concerned in forming the layout are to be called in at the stage of the first draft to express an opinion, depends on how independent the layout man is. A sketch will often lead both the copywriter and the photographer or artist to correct their ideas or adapt them to the other elements. However, if type and illustrations are ready in their final form, the layout man alone is responsible for weighing the relative importance of the elements involved and for seeing to it that they are satisfactorily placed. They form a foundation for the continuation of the work by the printers.

Essentially, the layout work of the art editor and the publication's make-up man is to co-ordinate the existing copy and illustrations, and to calculate and analyze the plan on which the printers can get to work.

Illus. 48—The character of lettering can also be changed by simple reversal. Widely contrasting effects are obtained, though the change is not always for the better. Symbols, trade-marks, etc., should be reversed with caution. In most cases, it is better to use them in unreversed form on a colored or screened background, if the usual form for some special reason is not desirable.

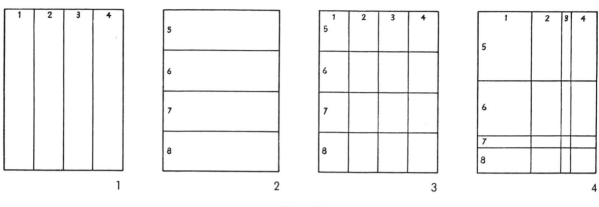

Illus. 49

The examples of layouts reproduced in this book are based on various preliminary fixed conditions, which are explained in the accompanying captions. Like the practical examples, they have been chosen and are discussed solely from the point of view of visual design and form. Their advertising value as far as content is concerned has not been examined, for it cannot be the function of a book on layout to judge the value or effectiveness of copy. (In fact, the text is often in a foreign language.)

In general, rectangular photographs and drawings should be indicated only by outlines; in the case of isolated photographs or drawn motifs—as is the practice in preliminary work—various procedures are adopted. The artistic ability of every layout man will decide the extent to which he will sketch in photographs or drawings in his layout. The more closely the layout approaches the expected final printed product, the better it will be for the layout man's colleagues and the client. The minimum requirement, in any event, is a drawing that will make it possible for everyone taking part to carry on with his job according to the measurements and shapes laid down.

DIVIDING AN AREA

With rare exceptions, the printed surface is a rectangle or a square. Most advertisements are based on rectangles. The problem is how to arrange copy and illustrations, or copy alone, in this space so as to make them interesting and exciting. The simplest division is made by halving; a vertical or horizontal line is drawn through the middle of the rectangle. If each of the new rectangles thus obtained is again halved in the same direction (Illus. 49), we obtain four equally wide and equally long strips (1 and 2). If we put these together, we get sixteen equally large rectangles (3). This division, however, looks monotonous and boring.

If we now push all or any of these lines closer, the result is a number of rectangles or squares of different sizes (4). They look somewhat livelier, but the whole has a restless appearance. It is obvious that this system of subdivision can also be started with only a single line, that oblique lines can also enhance tension, and that even curves, circles and ovals yield attractive subdivisions. However, we must be careful in layout when we make use of slanting lines, circles and parts of circles. It is important that every part obtained have an unambiguous form. A square must be a proper square and not nearly-a-square. A circle must be a real circle and not slightly oval. Parallels must not be almost-parallels. Every imperfect shape in the design is objectionable.

A framework of guide lines will help you to outline the individual units to be used in building up the layout: text and illustrations can be accommodated in these areas. This kind of division cannot be laid down as a standard, as it is not universally valid, but it helps to make creative work easier. Even in work apparently done without their aid, the presence of guide lines is suspected—they give stability and security to every layout. Other planning

60

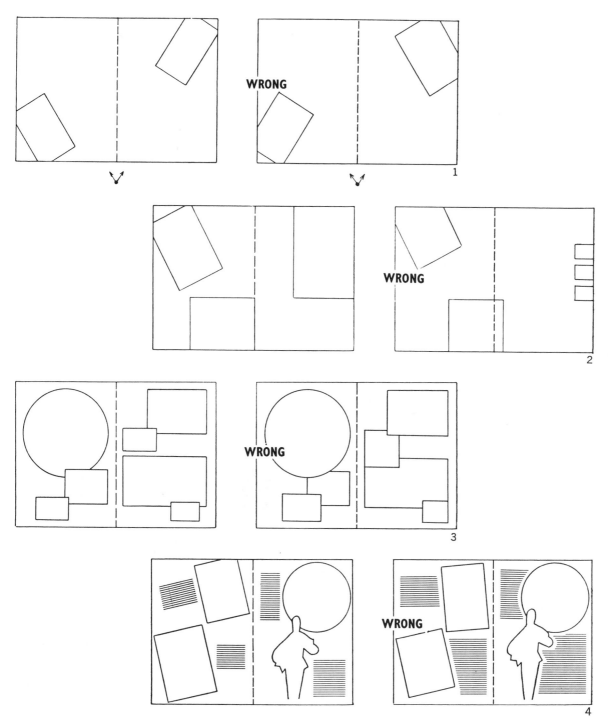

Illus. 50—Before deciding how to place illustrations it is important to take into account the following: Example 1. The reader is seated in the middle below the double page. All obliquely placed illustrations must be directed towards the middle, as otherwise they will "fall out" of the page. Edges, if cropped, must be cut in such a way that the size of the pictures can be perceived. Example 2. Large sizes gain in importance if they are "cut in." Do not allow pictures to cross the "gutter," the blank space in the middle two facing pages, as the parts generally print separately and seldom match exactly. Small cut-in illustrations on the edges look "squashed." Example 3. Smaller illustrations are always cut into larger ones. Large and small illustrations should never have edges in common. Example 4. Oblique or independently placed illustrations need breathing-space and should not be hemmed in either by other illustrations or by text. Ponderous illustrations should be placed as high up as possible on the pages, for the page will seem to be drooping if it is overweighted on the bottom half.

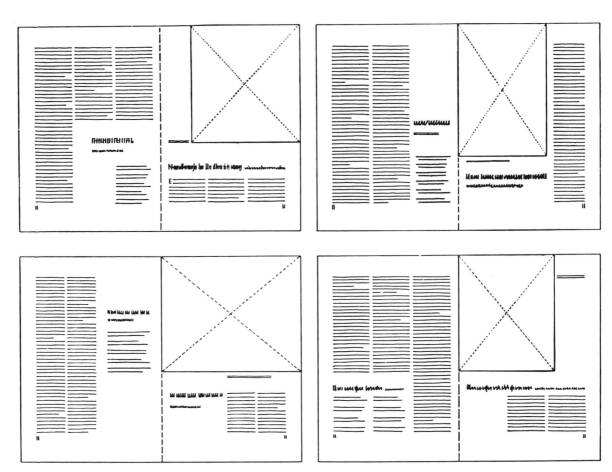

Illus. 51—Four ways of dealing with a double page that contains on the left the end of a story, a poem with a title, the author's name, and five two-liners; on the right, an illustration without definite measurements, the beginning of copy with a headline, and the author's name. Constructions with "corresponding" lines enable an agreeable calm to be achieved despite the varying elements. All these examples show the importance of white space for the structure and harmony of the double page.

methods can of course logically lead to good results, if the basic form is well marked.

If illustrations are to be worked into a layout, it is best to decide first on the approximate position and size of the most important ones, and then to extend the lines at the sides of the pictures to the edge of the entire layout. The guide lines (or margin lines) thus produced can be used—although they do not have to be—for the further development of the construction. They can enclose pictures, blocks of text, headings or white spaces according to their size and extent. No space should be packed full. White space, and nothing but white space, does full justice to black and to colors. Overloading advertisements with copy, illustrations and ornamentation is of no use to you or your clients.

DUMMYING PAGES

Planning an illustrated book, a magazine or newspaper, or such advertising literature as brochures, folders, catalogues and price lists, is very similar to the task of planning a book containing nothing but text. In these cases, too, the size must first be decided on. This is determined to some extent by the length of the text and the work that the illustrations have to do. There are four different ways of determining the order in which the further work should be carried out.

The text, the sizes of illustrations (if from earlier editions) and the length are often fixed. If this is the case, the possibility of bringing out the work in an entirely new format is restricted. As always, frequent changing of text widths

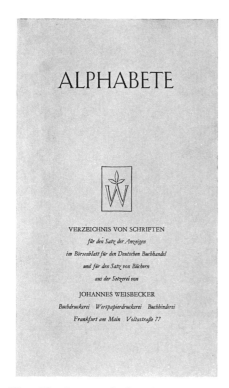

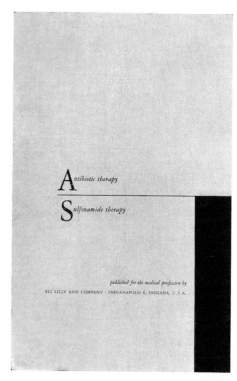

Illus. 52—Symmetrical and asymmetrical matter on the main title pages of specialized publications. Both are effective as a result of the clarity with which their different parts are distributed and their aristocratic unobtrusiveness.

should be avoided: the type matter should as far as possible run through the whole book in a uniform width. The width of the text can be decided on after the most frequent width of the illustrations has been noted. Illustrations narrower than the width of the type matter should be left to "float" inside the columns or be placed so that they run flush to the left or right edge of the columns, in other words, by using the principle of the guide lines. If there is enough room available, illustrations should never be packed tightly into the text matter, but given elbow room, for they are then more effective. Even if illustrations are placed in groups with white areas opposite or around them for contrast, the balance of black and white noted earlier should never be disturbed.

Illustrated pages become livelier if large illustrations are pushed out to the edge of the paper, outside the edge of the columns, to "bleed" off the page. Remember, if you bleed pictures, that at least $\frac{1}{8}$ of an inch will be trimmed off the photo, so allow for this in cropping your picture, in placement in the layout, and in the size of the page and sheet.

Let us say that you are ready to proceed. The text matter is set up in galley proofs and line plates have been made; that one-quarter of all the space will be occupied by illustrations and captions with proper white space. In addition, you have prepared the title page and preliminary pages (front matter), and all the special information (index, bibliography, etc.) for the back of the book. The remaining space is reserved for text. A set of galley proofs of the text, and engraver's proofs of the plates, are attached with corrections to go to the printer. A second set of proofs should be marked with page beginnings and endings, and a few sample pages pasted up. Pages with illustrations should each be dummied to show where they insert in the appropriate place. A memo about details and special layouts for the make-up man should be attached also to the pasted-up page dummy. This information is necessary if there is special work to be done, such as instructions regarding distances between columns, or distances between pictures or legends, or space above and below subheads (sideheads), etc.

63

Illus. 53—Four ways of dealing with a problem: One wide picture (proportions 5:4) as main illustration, and 7 tall ones (proportions 2.5:3.5) have to be placed on a double page with captions, headlines, and continuous text. The wide picture decides the face of the two pages and is therefore placed first. The guide lines emerging from it show the direction of construction. Title, text matter and captions are always placed so that the relationships between them are immediately apparent to the reader.

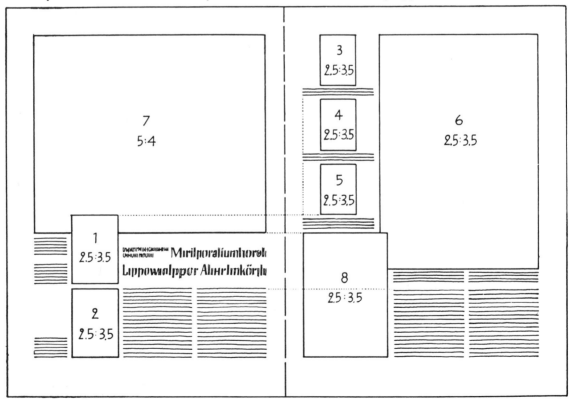

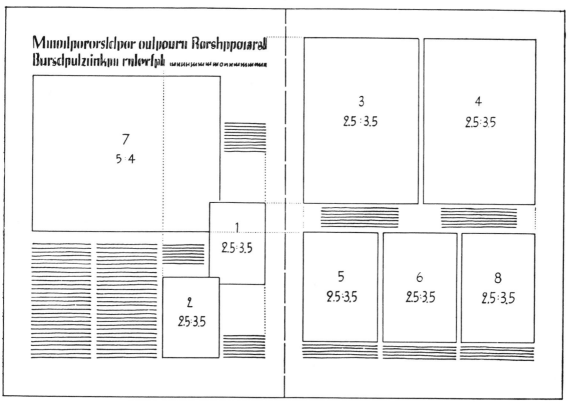

Illus. 54—Magazine pages and advertising literature should never be overloaded, for the eye needs occasional resting places. White areas—which, like illustrations and copy, should have clear outlines—ensure a well co-ordinated over-all impression. The distances between pictures, captions and texts should not be too varied, for this creates a restless appearance. A few emphatic differences, however, are always better than very small ones.

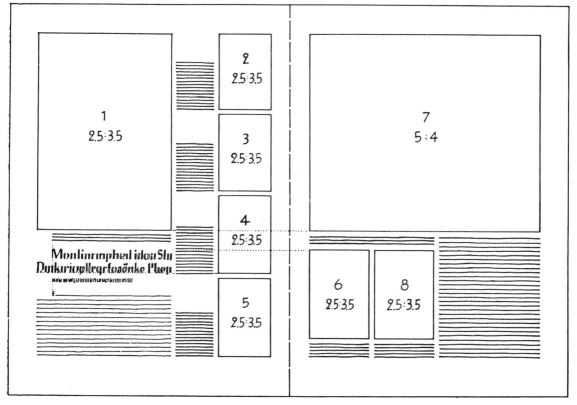

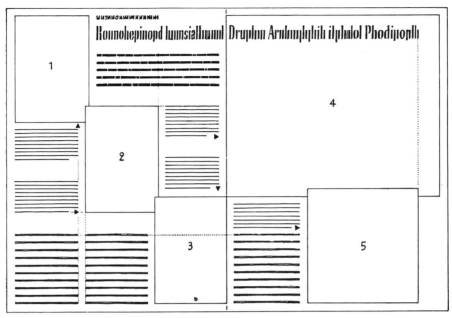

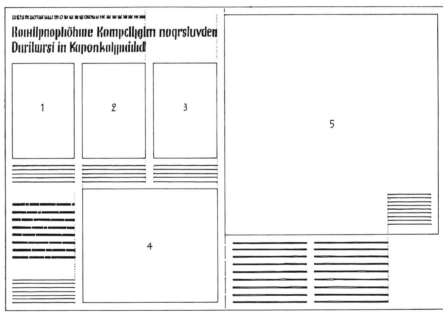

Illus. 55—Problem: To lay out a square picture, an oblong one (proportions 5:4) and 3 tall pictures (proportions 5:7) as well as a title, subtitle, matter and legends, on a definite type area. A printing process will be used with which it is possible to have text surprinted on illustrations. The surprinted text, however, must not conceal any essential part of the pictures. Solution: As most of the interest is in the pictures, it is best to keep a minimum of variation in the width of the columns and other measurements.

The manuscript can either be calculated ("copyfitted") in advance—type is set, and the position of the photo-engraved illustrations can be determined previously, or, if this method is time-wasting, uneconomical, and inexact, you can wait to make final layouts and dummy when the galley proofs come back.

If the length of a book is fixed, and the reading matter and the number of illustrations are known, the text matter must be calculated first (following the procedure on page 21), even when the illustrations are the most important part of the book. If the illustrations are to be placed independently of the text, it is possible

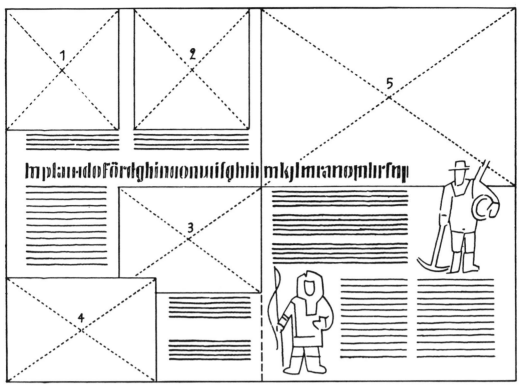

Illus. 56—Two ways of dealing with a double page containing 2 square pictures, 3 wide pictures (proportions 2:3) and two detached figures. The diagonal structure of the illustrations 4, 3 and 5 (above) is intercepted by the horizontals of the two squares and by the figures placed in the open.

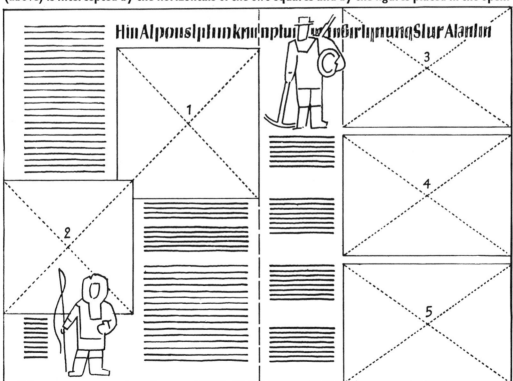

Illus. 57—Second solution: the large block of three illustrations on the right is loosened up by placing the captions on the left. The problem of the reading rhythm has been solved more effectively here than above, as the columns of text lie close together and are built up logically.

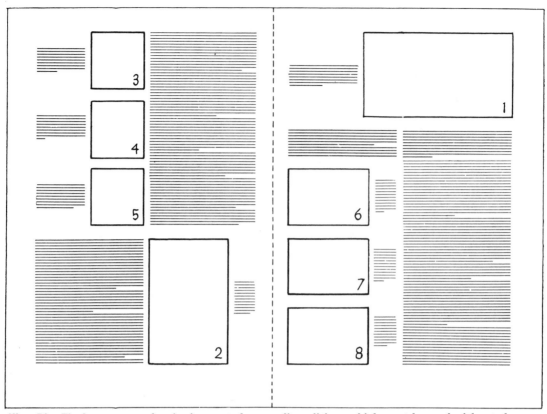

Illus. 58—The layout man often is given cuts from earlier editions which must be used without change. A different typeface and different column width can nevertheless provide new and interesting solutions to an advertising problem, as these examples show.

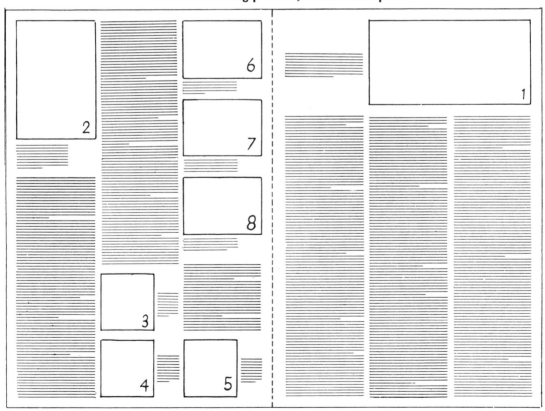

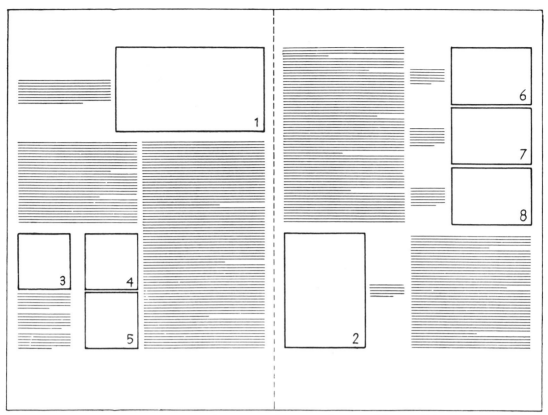

Illus. 59—Small illustrations can be advantageously grouped to provide a striking contrast to large sizes and blocks of matter. The area and shape of the paper has been used in varying ways in the examples of the problem solved here.

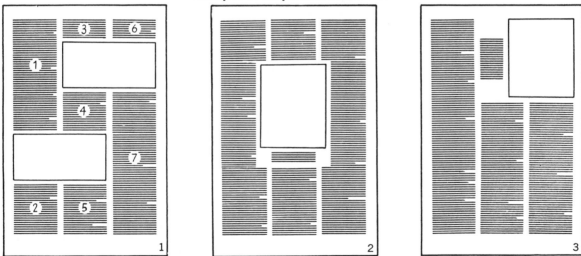

Illus. 60—(1) The reading rhythm of a page with pictures should always be uncomplicated, consistent and logical. It is a fundamental principle that the text should always begin with the left-hand column, even when the heading of a double page is for optical reasons not placed above that column (Illus. 55, top). The presence of illustrations does not change this rule, though in larger sizes the reading rhythm should not be too violently interrupted. (2) In placing illustrations, major attention must be paid, particularly in magazines, to the width of the column. Illustrations somewhat larger than the width of a column require a "run-around," a narrowing of column width, which usually looks inelegant. (3) Illustrations which are not as wide as two columns are best placed at the side, the rhythm of the column being maintained with the caption so that the reading flow is not interrupted.

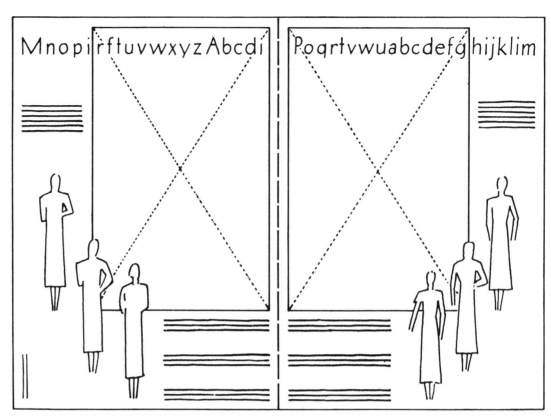

Illus. 61—Symmetrical and asymmetrical divisions of a double page in a fashion paper. As the picture content of fashion photographs is usually mobile, the structure of the layout should be restful and clear. Surprinting of copy over illustrations, most common in offset and gravure printing, must not adversely affect the pictorial motif.

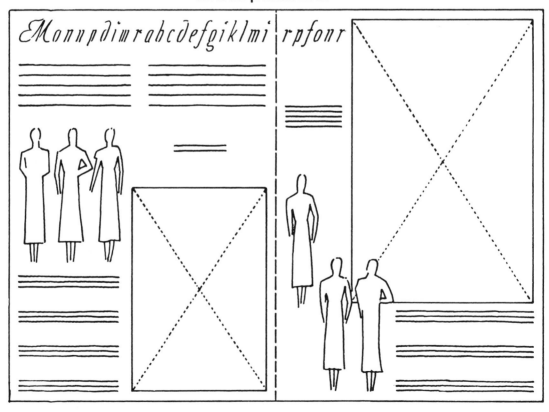

to use a free hand in deciding on the width of the text. But if the illustrations are to be placed in the text, it is advantageous to have the matter in two columns, for it is easier to work with narrow columns than with a single wide one. It is possible in this case to set only one column alone occasionally on a page, or two short columns, in order to make room for illustrations or to open up white space. Of course, it is also possible to vary the width of columns, although this usually is difficult to plan and it produces a discordant effect. Moreover, with machine-set type, alterations to page proofs are generally an expensive affair. If variations are desired, they should be effected in the illustrations, legends or captions, tables and footnotes. The front matter (title page, introduction, etc.) also will give an opportunity for special dramatic effects. When the length of the straight matter has been calculated, it is practical to paste it up in columns and fit in the illustrations as you dummy.

If you do not wish to fix on one or two or more columns first, but nevertheless want to know the overall length of the text matter, so that the sizes of the illustrations can be determined, calculate the size of the whole area to be occupied by the type first. Once the area for type and leading is determined, the number of letters in the manuscript can be divided by the number of letters per full line in various sizes of type. With each type size (and various leadings) you can allot the remaining space for the illustrations. As illustrations are far more variable and adaptable than type matter, their chief function should be to give life to the layout. Varying the sizes of illustrations will produce a far better effect than changing the widths of the type. The double-page examples given here illustrate various layout problems, and possible—though not the only possible— solutions of them.

In illustration layouts which are to be used by typesetter and compositor, the instructions for typesetting should be transferred immediately to the margin of the layout. In extensive jobs (even small ones) instructions should be written on a special specifications sheet. These can be repeated as they apply at difficult points in the manuscript, particularly where there is a change of width in the text, of the font (size of type) or the typeface used. A frequent change of fonts, such as is usual in legal documents, should be indicated by colored lines in the margin of the manuscript.

To facilitate work on the editorial side and in advertising departments, the printers provide both galley proofs and page pulls. These are generally placed side by side as double pages, in the case of books or magazines, the edges of the paper and column widths being printed in as dotted lines.

A typesetter might set up proofs of the job specifications on the first galley for everyone concerned. Essential information concerning illustrations for the photo-engravers should also be given on the "spec" sheet and copies made, so that inquiries and errors can be confirmed and rectified.

It is important that the layout man have contact with experienced personnel in the art department, and at the printer's and photo-engraver's who can understand and carry out his suggestions, and can follow up until the job is produced without having to make continuous inquiries. Some points of procedure can never be exhaustively explained, such as questions of spaces and indentions, retouching, surprinting, bleeding, etc.

In the planning of double pages as used in book printing, in magazines and in advertising media, such as brochures, folders, catalogues and house organs, it is obvious that almost all problems have at some time been more or less satisfactorily solved by good designers. We can therefore assume that your study of the problems will lead you to your own solutions. It is as important as studying the multiplication table to get all the experience you can by making use of all sources and all examples you can find, using the illustrations in this book as a springboard.

THE CHARACTER of any advertising medium must correspond essentially to what is being advertised. This applies above all to advertising media which make use of text, pictures and color, and which are generally produced and distributed in the form of printed matter.

The newspaper or magazine advertisement is the commonest means of approach to the buying public.

The package wrapper can be used for point-of-sale advertising and sales promotion, for it need not only serve, like the package, to contain a product. It can be an increasingly important means of advertising. Wrapper and package design will remain predominantly a matter for commercial art, but the layout man, typographer and photographer can help plan a selling wrapper.

The layout man is also needed to produce effective direct advertising: folders, brochures, catalogues, sales letters, newsletters, leaflets, handbills, price lists, calendars, house organs, and product bulletins.

In addition to these there are: the poster, which is intended to anchor a certain name, thing or product firmly in the subconscious by means of a powerful, emphatic appeal; the symbol, the starting point of advertising branded goods, and a sign of the unvarying quality of a product; and finally the large category of business stationery, which helps to define the image an enterprise presents to the world. Among the many other advertising media with visual appeal, are outdoor advertising, shop-window and exhibition design, film advertising, and various sales aids for the retail trade.

Even if an advertising piece's construction is entrusted at the start to but one guiding hand, many different forces contribute towards the shaping of the final design.

A uniform image with advertising value is obtained—particularly by those companies which appeal to a varied public—only by the use of a repeatedly presented symbol. Recently, however, with so many companies selling packaged goods, the package itself has increasingly tended to replace the brand symbol.

Since the package provides a potential for distinctive features in the form of text, shape and distinctive appearance, it is well equipped to make a direct appeal. The brand symbol often fails to put over the essential quality of the product, because it is so concentrated. But the package, like the brand symbol, must be a constant factor—it cannot be used for goods which follow the whims of fashion.

With the publication advertisement, the situation is different. It is versatile and adaptable and can speak to the reader in ever-new ways. But, if it is not to lose his interest, it needs an eye-catching feature—the name of the product, the manufacturer, an illustrated brand symbol or package or some other well-defined and unmistakable final chord. One of the most important tasks of the layout man is to develop the advertisement's active appealing elements and to bring them into an effective relationship with each other.

THE ADVERTISEMENT ITSELF

The newspaper and magazine advertisement takes pride of place in commercial advertising. Its advantages are relatively low cost in relation to the great number of potential buyers who can be influenced, the precisely defined distribution areas, the wide range of readership, the possibility of well-timed appearance and of adapting word and picture to publication date. The fact that the appeal and its design can be shaped to fit just the circle of readers it is desired to approach (dailies, weeklies,

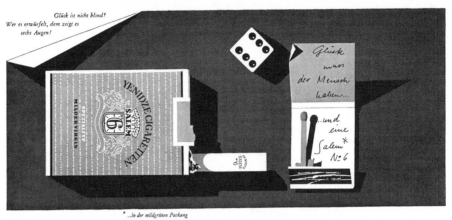

Glück muss der Mensch haben . . . und eine Salem Nº 6 *(Milder Virgin)*

Illus. 62—An advertising page need lose none of its vitality even if it makes use of only a limited number of motifs, as shown by this advertisement for Salem cigarettes. The cigarettes and their pack are supplemented only by matches and dice, but no individual features are forfeited. Getting the utmost out of a minimum of creative factors demands great skill in construction and in placing the shapes used.

monthlies, trade papers) offers unique opportunities for direct sales action. In addition, there is the possibility of effective repetition, daily or weekly, on readers.

Advertisements vary greatly in format and appearance, and new forms of design are continually turning up, yet the building units used remain largely the same. The following features can appear in an advertisement, but they are not indispensable:

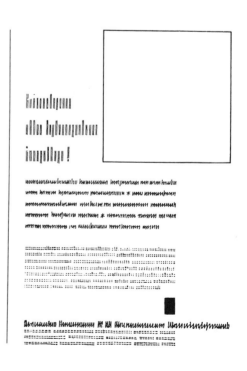

Illus. 63—Four layout drawings for a publication advertisement. Supplied are a square photograph, a heading with attached text, text copy, symbol, and the company's name and address. Above, left, is a symmetrical construction, usable provided the picture has no eccentric "inner life" of its own. The effect is distinguished. Asymmetrical solutions (above, right) to layout problems provide more opportunities for variety. The guidance given to the eye in the advertisement on the left below is full of tension if the pictorial theme is interesting enough to bridge the space between headline and text. The brand symbol, acting as a counterpoise to the illustration in both layouts below, provides a further powerful accent. Try to manage with as few typefaces and type sizes as possible. No advertisement should resemble a book of typeface specimens.

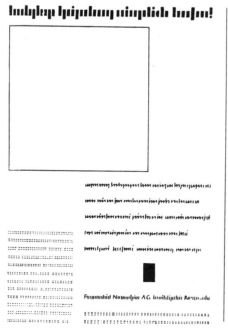

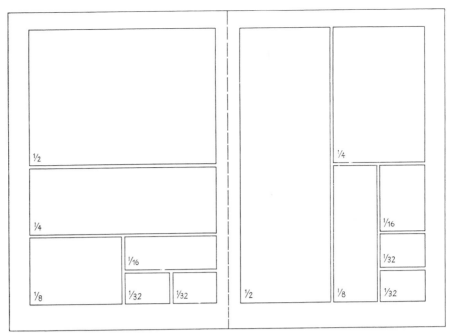

Illus. 64—Division of an advertising page in a newspaper or magazine to accommodate small display advertisements (as small as 1/32 of a page). There are generally eight columns on ad pages in newspapers with full-size pages. To make a more forceful subdivision than is illustrated here, or to lay out a page with more small advertisements containing pictures and text, always involves a risk that the whole page-picture will be spoiled by the "bad eggs" among the advertisements. Classified ads are another story.

• Headline, as prelude to or as the initial phase of the advertisement.

• Text, with its various functions and subdivisions.

• Information about the advertiser.

• Picture material, which may be dominant, independent or illustrative.

• Brand (verbal or symbolic)—and also the slogan, with its unvarying appeal or catch-phrase.

• Coupon, if direct-by-mail response is wanted.

• Decorative additions, borders, etc., which give the advertisement its distinctive note or set it apart from its rivals.

The external image of an advertisement is determined by the tasks it has to fulfil. The nature of the appeal determines the strength and position to be given to every part. It follows that the design of the layout must be the result of an advertising plan (perhaps the result of a conference, or part of a campaign), and that a decision has been made regarding the theme or leading idea on which the series

of advertisements, or of the single advertisement, is based.

The chief task of the layout man, therefore, is to work with ready-made copy, to design it, perhaps supply illustrations, and thus provide an individual countenance. Start with the picture. It attracts attention more quickly and with more lasting effects than pure text. As it is easier to adapt text to picture than vice versa, the picture should always be given priority as a creative element. This does not mean that it will transcend the text in importance, but treat it as an eye-catcher intended to attract attention and to induce the viewer to read.

However, to use a picture merely for illustrating a text or headline is to deprive it of much of its proper function. To use a picture simply to catch the reader's eye, without any reference to the text, is also risky. The easy leap from picture to text intended by the advertiser may not be successfully made. It may not even be attempted. If a picture simply illustrates or "underpaints" the printed word,

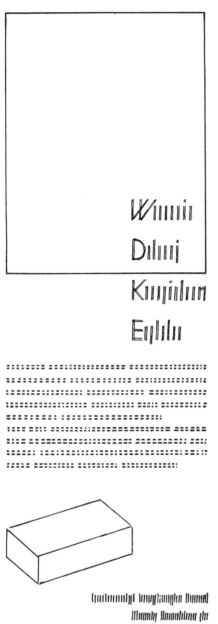

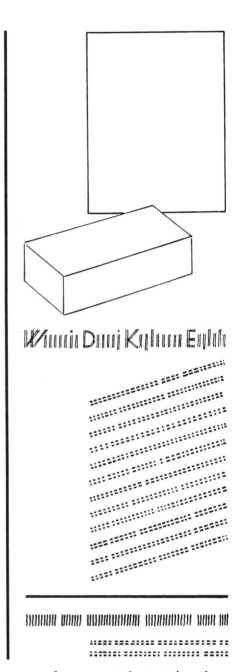

Illus. 65—Two layouts for a publication advertisement with a top picture, a package, heading, text, and information about the advertiser. On the left, the package supplies a counterpoise to the well spaced heading which links the picture to the text. The perspective lines of the package in the layout on the right are repeated in the slanting text. The advertisement must not appear on the left-hand border of the page, as it is too open on the left.

it does no more than repeat the text in other terms, and it can of course do much more than that. The proper sequence is to make the eye complete a comfortable movement from one element to the other, from words to picture or from picture to words.

Photography, making steady progress towards technical perfection, has become a universal means of pictorial expression. Nevertheless, using a photo involves a danger. The abundance of good photographs, the sophisticated effects that every photographer can obtain nowadays from the simplest subjects, can blunt

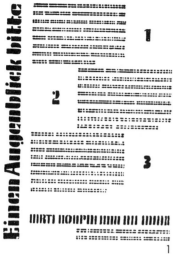

Illus. 66—Not always does one realize that small advertisements also need air if they are to do their job well and assert themselves among their usually overloaded companions. It is more important here than anywhere else to be different from the rest, to stand out from the others. These layouts are effective only if a clear type is used, one that flows easily even if it is compressed, so that the build-up of the lines is not destroyed by separations. In all these examples, the three blocks of text ensure a powerful appeal. The symmetry of No. 2 may seem to make it conventional, but the triple border provides an excellent shield against adjoining advertisements. In small ads, carefully chosen text with irreproachable typefaces is indispensable. Nos. 2, 3 and 4 can be placed anywhere; No. 1 is a left-hand advertisement; Nos. 5 and 6 must stand on the right.

the viewer's perceptive faculties so that he is becoming incapable of appreciating unique quality when he sees it. The widespread lack of a color sense makes most people uncritically receptive to bad color-photographs, and renders it difficult to find a clear path towards greater utilization of color in photographic advertising.

Even if you have available the best mechanically produced photograph, this cannot lessen the value of using creative art. The sheer uniqueness of a drawing, the fact that it has been shaped by human hands, the vast number of techniques available in reproduction, are all factors that make art valuable for advertising purposes. If the photograph is more effective as reportage, for quick news presentation, if it strikes home because of its immediacy and its veracity, real or apparent, the drawing is surer in its aim than a photograph can ever be. Only art can completely eliminate the non-essential and simplify the subject so much that a pure concentration of the atmosphere is actually achieved. Art succeeds in following the mental processes of the advertiser more clearly than

Es sieht fast wie ein Alphorn aus,
indessen der Helveter
trank manchmal einen Schluck daraus
(das Glas erfand man später).

Bis in die allerhöchsten Kreise
Löscht man den Durst in gleicher Weise
Hier haben Hoheit Seine Gnaden
Zu einem Trunke eingeladen.

Der Kenner edler Kunst genießt,
Daß sie nicht leere Schönheit ist.
An diesem feinen langen Glas
Macht Form sowohl wie Inhalt Spaß.

Aber schon damals wußte man:

Das Zeitalter der Tafelfreuden wußte:

Besonders wenn es Bier ist, denn:

Illus. 67—Three small advertisements issued jointly by Swiss breweries. The vignettes are realistically drawn with a humorous touch re-echoed in the text. Words and pictures, like the slogan, radiate shirtsleeved ease and well-being and make a direct appeal to the heart of the thirsty reader. (Design by R. Gilsi, Switzerland.)

the photograph can, it is more condensed and more human, it can adapt itself more easily than the photograph to the text—which of course is itself based on a design that was originally drawn.

If you are undecided whether to use photographs or drawings in an advertisement, first make up your mind whether the picture is to provide a foil for the text or to conform to and agree with it. There are also of course technical considerations to be taken into account. A photograph intended to be effective because of its wealth of grey tones is not in its right place on newsprint. But gravure printing in a magazine satisfies all the essential conditions for printing a good photograph. As most advertisers in illustrated publications work with photographs, use eye-catching ones—as distinct from purely factual photographs—but use them with caution, because your competitors for the reader's eye will as a rule also be using them.

The most important maxim, therefore, is "Be different!"—an injunction that should always be remembered for every advertisement. For a little while it may be pleasanter and easier to swim in the wake of successful fellow-advertisers or let yourself be drawn by the same currents that have taken them to success, but the fact that you have been copying other

people's ideas will soon become obvious, and if the worst comes to the worst it may even involve you in trouble with the law. The reported sales figures of other advertisers should never lead you to follow blindly along the path that took them to success. Remember that a successful piece of work always has a disreputable queue of plagiarizers behind it. Carried to its logical conclusion—and the tendency does exist—new ideas are worked to death until the final result is uniformity. In advertising, more than anywhere else, it is the new and uncopied that proves most effective. Appeals are like knives: used too much, they become blunt. Unusualness and freshness are best.

Pictures, both photographs and art, realistic and symbolic, if they have mobility, contain values that appeal to the feelings even when unaided by accompanying text. The more directly and immediately a picture appeals to the observer, the more powerful is the impulse. If a realistic form is artistically transposed by reinterpretation and simplification, cast into another form which is not so easy to interpret, its emotional content is diminished and intellect takes over, until the former disappears entirely. If you are advertising desserts or baby foods, you will need an easily "readable" picture both in the advertisement itself and in

Illus. 68—Humorous appeals always find attentive readers. Anthropomorphized animals, when the artist has a positive approach to both their human and non-human elements, are always looked at with pleasure, as the success of Walt Disney's films show. The package is designed to attract shoppers in supermarkets. The company's name stands on its own and conspicuously at the base; a colored edge finishes off the front of the box, and underlines the repeated name like a ribbon when the goods are stacked.

Illus. 69—A Swiss company in Berne published a little book of recipes with vividly colored photographs of dishes opposite practical typography on the text pages. The alternation of bold and light is, of course, by no means unusual, but is seldom worked out so effectively. The Clarendon typeface of the headlines harmonizes with the Garamond of the text.

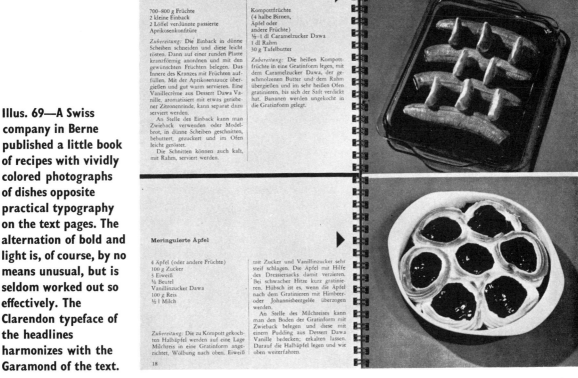

Illus. 70—The hands are important, and they derive their significance not only from the subject of the advertisement (food), but also from the way they are drawn and placed. The left hand guides the eyes from the slogan over the text to the package. The two rectangles are at just the point where the left hand is placed symmetrically in relation to the right. The fingers point like arrows to the package, whose shadow connects the figure of the chef (who is pointing to the price) with the end of the text. The open construction of text and picture makes the essential elements—the black-and-white drawings and the package—appear still more clearly outlined and condensed.

every other illustrated accessory used (the picture on the package, for instance). If you are selling medical preparations to doctors, you can make use of a summarized, concise form with an abstract content. You can be sure that any doctor will understand the purport of a printed synthesis as easily as he can read the chemical formula of a drug.

Pictures reinforce every verbal argument. Most people are visual types, seeking and finding their way with their eyes; they look for illustrated offers, because copy alone, however good it may be, communicates no conclusive ideas to them.

The second, only occasionally used, pictorial appeal in an advertisement is its setting. It should never work by itself alone; it must serve the purposes of the other formal elements. Usually it sets off an advertisement from adjacent displays, but it must also—particularly in rows of advertisements—be consistently carried out and accentuate the uniform character of these.

The headline, whether placed independently or supported and amplified by the picture, demands not only consummate word sense

Illus. 71—The elegantly poised and airily placed hand supports the theme, but serves even more as a pointer to it. The white threads on the varied grey surfaces emphasize what is being offered. The subject is shopping, and the magazine's aim is to help shoppers find what they want. The free treatment of the text provides an effective contrast to the cool outlines of the drawing. (Design by G. Federico.)

but good graphic design also. The longer a headline is, the less eccentric or extraordinary its typeface should be, for distinctive quality is effective only when concentrated. Long rows of capitals or accumulations of fantastically shaped letters make for poor readability. As a rule, script types make a good contrast to text matter. Because of their wealth of ascenders and descenders and their mobile line-arrangement, they are always full of tension, whether placed horizontally or slightly aslant, written smoothly with a pen or roughly with a dry brush. Usually the text following the headline is an emotionally accentuated continuation of the appeal. It should therefore differ from the factual text in the form and arrangement of types used.

The text proper, if it does not simply consist of a few sentences, should be appropriately divided up so that distinct concepts are more clearly separated and the reading rhythm led more easily in the right direction.

The slogan which supports or replaces the company symbol must be clearly placed apart from the rest of the text.

The trade-mark and the name of the company should be adapted to the purpose the advertisement has to serve. The weight of the name must never conflict with the drawn or set slogan. Care should be taken that if the slogan and the trade-mark or company name appear in similar kinds of type, as for example, two italic typefaces, there should be a *strong* contrast.

Coupons are often too small, so that they are overlooked and fail to serve their purpose.

Illus. 72—Charmingly caricatured and therefore enticing are the figures on these two advertisements. The visual guide lines created by the drawings are important. While the dynamic triangle of the construction on the left passes from the bird cage above the girl's bent knee to the eye-catching point of her black underwear and back to the trade-mark, the movement in the right-hand version is reversed: guided by the extended knee, the eye stops again at the trade-mark. Headline and slogan frame the graceful play of lightly and freely running lines in Roman type.

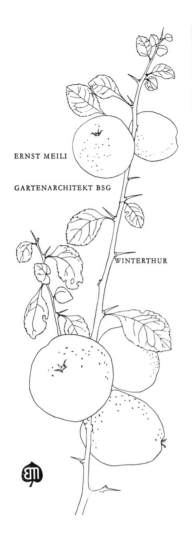

ERNST MEILI

GARTENARCHITEKT BSG

WINTERTHUR

Illus. 73—(Left) The surprise effect of a delicately delineated illustration in the advertising pages of a periodical is particularly great if the adjacent advertisements make use of a more striking, cruder method of presentation. Against curves and counter-movements and the vital interior drawing of the leaves and fruits, the rigidity of the few lines of print offers a really expressive contrast. The individual mark of the landscape designer, who is the advertiser in this case, is the exactly placed symbol near the base of the advertisement.

Illus. 74—(Right) The cognac advertisement uses stronger contrasts. The product and its most famous connoisseur are well placed in relation to each other by the use of clear symbols. The ensemble is well thought out graphically also: movement and counter-balance are excellently attuned to each other.

Cognac impérial

Or du cognac dans le cristal des verres... Luminosité du ciel de Charente... Où donc ailleurs que sur cette terre de France pourrait naître la plus parfaite des eaux de vie? Ame ardente du vin, le Cognac est un don privilégié de la nature: Courvoisier est fier de vous offrir son Cognac, œuvre d'art exceptionnelle qu'il façonne avec amour et qui trouve avec honneur sa place sur les tables souveraines. Le Cognac Courvoisier, au riche bouquet et au parfum rare...

V.S.O.P.

COURVOISIER

The Brandy of Napoleon

COGNAC
COURVOISIER

Jean Haecky Importation S. A. Bâle

They should be placed so that the reader can easily and conveniently cut them out.

Before the advertisement is planned, it is important to know what kind of printing, paper and screens for letterpress or offset are to be used. Also try to find out the number of different newspapers in which the advertisement is to appear in the same form. If a layout has to be made for several newspapers or magazines of different sizes, it is practical to design the advertisement for the smallest size first. It can then be adapted for the larger sizes without heavy additional expense, by simply placing the small layout on the larger area, dividing it up into its component formal elements, "exploding" them and recomposing them in a looser form. Proofs of a sample of the smaller advertisement are better to cut out and place

anew. If matrices, stereos or electrotypes are to be used, you must content yourself with simply a more open placement if the sizes are different, or a new setting will have to be made.

In the case of texts for illustrated publications printed in offset, intaglio, or gravure you can use reproduction proofs of the text, pulled on fast-white paper, and paste in your picture material. Different sized advertisements can be equalized by separating the formal parts of the layout and putting them together again in a new paste-up.

If you are anxious to have your advertisements retain an individual cast, and ensure that their special quality will be consistently maintained, it is not advisable to hand the problem over to a newspaper composing-room, even if instructions are clear and you have

Warum

die Schönheit fliehen lassen?

Bewahren Sie sich doch, wie Tausende von Frauen, die zarte Schönheit jugendfrischer Haut. Gönnen auch Sie sich täglich die BOTANA-Natur-Hautpflege. Dann wird jeder den mattschimmernden Schmelz Ihres blütenreinen Teints bewundern.

BOTANA, komponiert aus hauterneuernden Kräutern, schönheitsfördernden Wirkstoffen und Vitamin F – eine Spitzenleistung wissenschaftlich fundierter Kosmetik.

Natürliche Schönheit verleiht Ihnen die BOTANA-Natur-Hautpflege auf Kräuterbasis - sie läßt die Haut nicht nur jung erscheinen -, sie verjüngt sie tatsächlich und schenkt ihr Zartheit und Frische. Nie sollten Sie vergessen, vor jeder Creme-Behandlung die Haut mit BOTANA-Tonic, dem milden, belebenden Gesichtswasser, zu reinigen.

Eine Probepackung BOTANA-Cremes mit Kräuteressenzen und Vitamin F erhalten Sie kostenlos; schreiben Sie bitte an die Lingner Werke Düsseldorf, Fichtenstr. 54

BOTANA-Tonic ab DM 2.20
BOTANA-Nährcreme DM 2.40
BOTANA-Halbfettcreme DM 2.40
BOTANA-Tagescreme DM 2.40

Botana

ungewöhnlich und sehr sehr gut

Sie werden mit dem Erfolg zufrieden sein! Andernfalls erhalten Sie, bei Einsendung der angebrochenen Packung an die Lingner Werke, den Kaufpreis zurück.

Illus. 75—Two advertisements in a series. The varying treatment and placing of the pictorial elements provide different reading-rhythms. On the left, the distinctive profile is freely placed and connected by the hand with the flower and thence to the product. Headline, text and name make up the counter-rhythm. On the right, the girl's face is placed on a quiet background. It thus loses some of its individual quality, but to the advantage of the product, which are points of guidance for the text. The layout is friendlier and more intimate than the more compact design on the left, which has more coolly placed elements.

Machen Sie's doch ebenso!

Kennen Sie das Rezept vieler Frauen, die man um ihre Schönheit beneidet? „Alle Tage mit BOTANA!" Machen Sie's doch ebenso! Gönnen Sie sich täglich die BOTANA-Natur-Hautpflege. So erfüllt sich Ihr Wunsch nach strahlender Frische und jugendlichem Charme.

BOTANA, komponiert aus hauterneuernden Kräutern, schönheitsfördernden Wirkstoffen und Vitamin F – eine Spitzenleistung wissenschaftlich fundierter Kosmetik.

Natürliche Schönheit verleiht Ihnen die BOTANA-Natur-Hautpflege auf Kräuterbasis - sie läßt die Haut nicht nur jung erscheinen -, sie verjüngt sie tatsächlich und schenkt ihr Zartheit und Frische. Nie sollten Sie vergessen, vor jeder Creme-Behandlung die Haut mit BOTANA-Tonic, dem milden, belebenden Gesichtswasser, zu reinigen.

Eine Probepackung BOTANA-Cremes mit Kräuteressenzen und Vitamin F erhalten Sie kostenlos; schreiben Sie bitte an die Lingner Werke Düsseldorf, Fichtenstr. 57

BOTANA-Tonic ab DM 2.20
BOTANA-Nährcreme DM 2.40
BOTANA-Halbfettcreme DM 2.40
BOTANA-Tagescreme DM 2.40

Botana

ungewöhnlich und sehr sehr gut

Sie werden mit dem Erfolg zufrieden sein! Andernfalls erhalten Sie, bei Einsendung der angebrochenen Packung an die Lingner Werke, den Kaufpreis zurück.

---

supplied a layout. The newspaper will use any machine-set or hand-set typefaces available. It is far better to entrust a typesetting house with the assignment. Here, your type specifications will be followed exactly and later you can make stereos, electrotypes or prints for intaglio or offset printing. All the materials needed for final insertion will be supplied by them. Typesetting specialists have good modern typefaces on hand and generally show sympathetic understanding of the wishes of their customers in everything concerning advertising and layout work.

In designing advertisements with or without illustrations, it is important to do more than *approximate* calculation. A free and mobile arrangement of lines, often successfully used in contrast to blocks of type, is a way of giving the type picture more life, and also of removing small errors of calculation. But allowing a margin for expansion is not really sufficient. Every word and every space between words should be counted, and if the text is tight, it may even be necessary to make a drawing of the entire text, word by word, in order to ensure that the intended effect can be judged and appreciated. Careful methods of arrangement are welcome not only from the point of view of design: they serve, as in poetry, to secure an intelligible separation into distinct contexts without disturbing hyphenations.

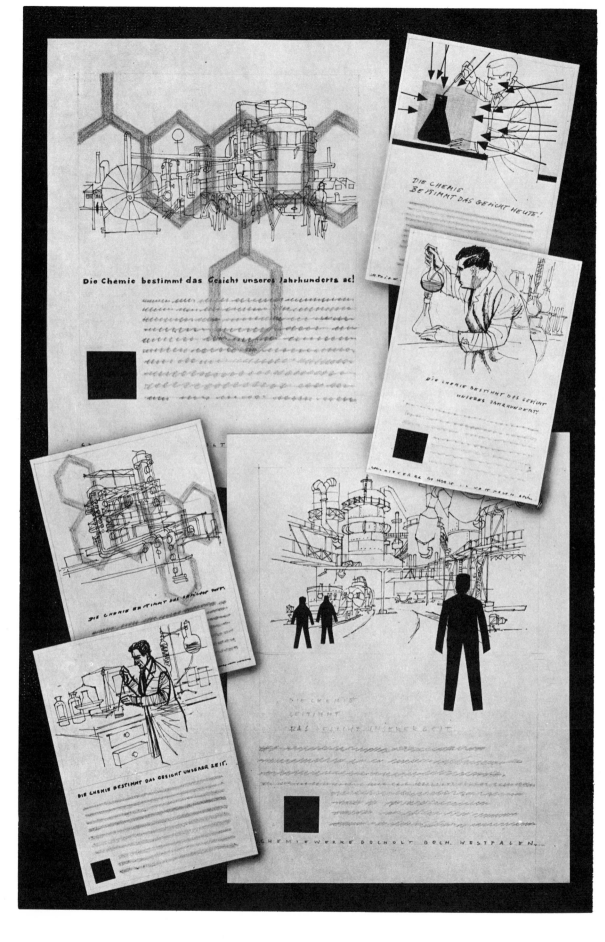

Die Chemie bestimmt das Gesicht unserer Zeit!

 Jahrtausende hindurch stürmte der Mensch vorwärts, getrieben von dem unstillbaren Drang, mehr zu wissen, besser zu leben. Seine Erfahrungen gab er von Generation zu Generation weiter. Er lernte es, seine physische Stärke durch von ihm entdeckte und entwickelte Mechanismen zu vervielfachen oder zu ersetzen, er schaltete Energien ein, die das Antlitz der Erde umformten. Er wurde Herr über Naturvorgänge und Gewalten und machte sich Kräfte zunutze, die ihm halfen, leichter und gefahrloser zu schaffen. Seine Forderungen an die Umwelt wurden immer größer, seine Ansprüche an die Perfektion alles ihm Dienenden führten zu immer neuen Bemühungen, zu neuen Industrien und Wirtschaftszweigen. Die Sorge um die Erhaltung des Erreichten zwang ihn neue Wege zu erschließen, um jenen Anforderungen gerecht werden zu können. So entstand ein wesentlicher Zweig der Chemiewirtschaft, die Reinigungstechnik. Die Chemiewerke Bocholt stellen Grundstoffe, Halbfabrikate und Endprodukte für alle Wirtschaftszweige her, die Reinigungsaufgaben zu lösen haben.

Chemiewerke Bocholt Bocholt in Westfalen Stephanstraße 44-52 Ruf Sammelnummer 377

Illus. 76—Quick sketches offer solutions of various kinds to an advertising problem. The sketch at the lower right of the page opposite was chosen for the final, though it still required some alterations in the theme of the picture and in the structure of the text. The customer's layout with pasted-in matter was provided. The striking figures in the foreground, mere symbols, have had their relative positions carefully chosen. They give depth to the picture by leading the eye to the line drawing of the industrial plant. (Drawings by Peter Matthes.)

**die revolutionierenden
Wollechtfarbstoffe,
ergeben auch bei stark
gedrehten Garnen
und dicht geschlagenen
Geweben einwandfreie
Färberesultate**

Irgalane

Kurze Färbedauer und ungewöhnliches Durch-
dringungsvermögen! Diese beiden scheinbar
gegensätzlichen Eigenschaften finden sich in
den Irgalanen in idealer Weise vereinigt. Dazu
bieten diese Farbstoffe den Vorteil, in jedem
Fall Färbungen von hervorragenden Echtheiten
zu ergeben, wie sie sich nur mit den besten
Chromierungsfarbstoffen erzielen lassen.

J. R. Geigy A.G., Basel

Illus. 77—A colored supplement to a periodical issued by a Swiss chemical company making dyes. The lively illustrated subjects produce an especially striking effect in juxtaposition to the circles, which are divided up in accordance with a harmonious color scheme. The triangle formed by the pictures together with the name provides tension. The arrangement of the lines in the text results naturally from the subdivisions of the geometrical elements. The guide lines are very easily recognizable in this advertisement.

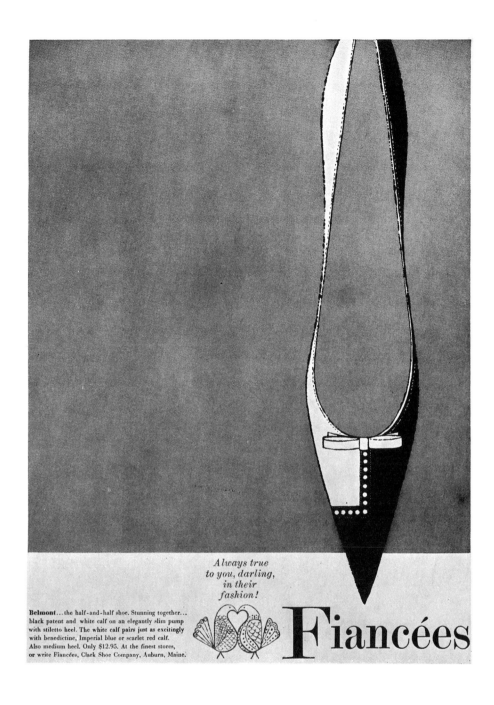

*Always true
to you, darling,
in their
fashion!*

Belmont...the half-and-half shoe. Stunning together...
black patent and white calf on an elegantly slim pump
with stiletto heel. The white calf pairs just as excitingly
with benedictine, Imperial blue or scarlet red calf.
Also medium heel. Only $12.95. At the finest stores,
or write Fiancées, Clark Shoe Company, Auburn, Maine.

Fiancées

Illus. 78—An unusual advertisement; in fact, hardly more than a
simple statement of fact. This announcement in a fashion paper, with
its economical three-fold color scale of black, white and grey, shows
distinction and thus appeals to the sensibilities of a minority who
appreciate such advertising. Good printing is essential for the effectiveness of such an advertisement. The probing glance is caught by the
vertical, and led to the name.

Illus. 79—Differences in the sizes of advertisements require a client to provide various layouts of the same copy and illustrations, so that the available advertising space will be utilized fully. The general impression produced by the basic form should remain unchanged in each of the variations, however. As the text is more easily adaptable than the illustration, it is usually the former that is changed and made to fit the picture. The most unforced and individual solutions are those in which the graphic artist has the freedom to reduce the size of the illustration without impairing its effect. (All advertisements have been reduced in the same scale.)

Illus. 80—The startling impact of this advertisement is obtained by the repeated copying of a negative showing a television picture tube. It is not only the product itself with its distinctive outlines and its repetition that is compulsive, but also the rhythm of the novel inner contours arising out of the reduplicated picture. The mobile-like silhouette of the whole has enough white space around it; the text accompanies the pattern without disturbing it. The smoothly flowing reading-rhythm from top to bottom ends in the name of the company. (Anton Stankowski.)

Illus. 81—(Left) This colored Kodak advertisement in a Swiss magazine proves that a clear distinction between ideas to be expressed need not lead to a break between the different graphic units used. The realistic photograph supplies information just as the text does, while the heading and the drawing communicate atmosphere. There is color only in the drawing. It frames the product, links it with great advertising effectiveness to the symbols of Christmas and thus turns the thoughts to wishes and gifts. Intentionally, the tree bough points both to the heading and to the camera. The position of the strings reminds one of the lines sometimes surprinted on photographs of cameras in catalogues and technical publications, to identify the various parts of the apparatus.

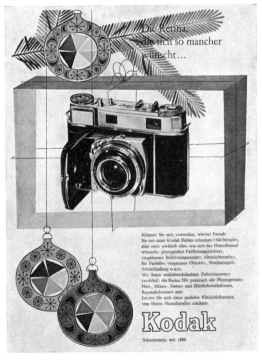

Illus. 82—A realistic and generally naturalistic form of illustration must be used for foods, products for everyday use, and everything intended to conquer the housewife's heart. If you know how to assemble and arrange articles in a drawing or a photograph so that the subjects will increase the tension of the advertisement, you will never fail to find good ways of solving advertising problems. The rolled slices of ham are not only appetizing; pictorially, too, they are effectively grouped. They point to the head-line, to the text, and to the recipe, and lead the eye back to themselves again and again.

Illus. 83—The Armour advertisement is overloaded: the picture sections are placed too close together in a bewildering relationship of sizes. Hunt's advertisement on the other hand is admirably balanced. Both these graphically designed layouts follow photographic themes. Everything non-essential has been eliminated. With a trend towards packaged products, advertisers increasingly demand photographers and graphic artists who can solve the problem of showing packages effectively in all advertising media.

A Dry Martini—to deserve the name—must be a happy blend of *two* ingredients. Use enough of the new Noilly Prat French Vermouth to make its *civilizing* presence felt! Pale, but not pallid—extra dry and light *by nature*—Noilly Prat makes a *vital* difference in your cocktails. Don't ever stir without it!

BROWNE VINTNERS CO., INC., NEW YORK, N. Y. • SOLE DISTRIBUTORS FOR THE U. S. A.

Illus. 84—(Above) Common to all the advertisements of this chemical firm is a yellow background, relieved by white open spaces and drawings. There is a strong contrast between the powerful verticals of the mast with its crosspieces, the text blocks and the small pictures that accentuate the horizontals. The lineman's distinctive outlines stress his independence from this strict opposition of contrasting elements, and form magnetic points, together with the firm's symbol, which stands apart from the whole. The division of the text provides for breathing spaces and at the same time encourages the viewer to read. (Design by Roland Rodegast.)

Illus. 85—(Left). Eye-catching advertisements—even without slogans and appeals—often have an explosive yet ineffective action because they reveal no clear connection with the text. In this case, however, the space is well filled with an exciting pictorial design, and the two hands holding the glasses point to the unusually placed slogan. The reader's eyes move from there without check, and each line of the text ends at the bottles. "Spirit"—in both senses of the word—and "esprit" are cognate words. This is an advertisement that "arrives."

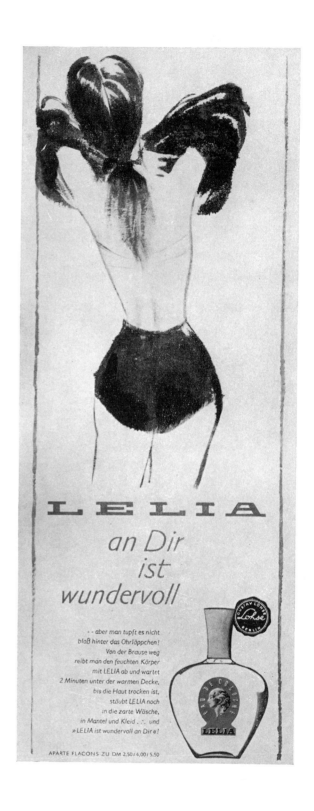

Illus. 86—The superiority of the drawing to the photograph is manifest in fashion advertising, which often gives beauty its due far more thoroughly than a photograph of a model. (Design by Otto Glaser.)

Illus. 87—The Opel advertisement is striking even without the attractive coloring of the original. The picture is more than an illustration of the text: it says what is essential without words. The unusualness of the design arouses attention. Images evoked by the feathers, the wheel, and the leather driving glove—lightness, technical excellence, and exclusiveness—are conjured up more rapidly and effortlessly than any text can be read. The hand arrests the reader's eye, which passes easily from the feathers to the wheel, and thence to the name of the car.

Illus. 88a—The hard black and white of a greatly enlarged halftone, and its impressive contours, furnish a successful contrast to the delicate lines of the photographed feathers, in pastel brown and blue. While the feathers are cropped in as a supplementary pattern, the Indian's head has ample breathing space. The separation of the parts obeys the rules an art editor has to observe when he is deciding how to crop portraits.

Illus. 88b—Here the work of the photographer is directed and defined by the rhythm followed in the distribution of themes. The inclined figures, swaying as if striving towards the headline, are pleasurably exciting. The vital content of the illustrations enjoys ample freedom in the light-colored rectangles. The triple picture is refreshing and ebullient. The text finds continuation and conclusion in the lower illustrations.

Illus. 89—More proof that drawings make it easier for readers to identify themselves with a figure or a happening, by giving freer run to the fantasy than photographs, which leave nothing unsaid. The fashion drawing here charmingly exaggerates and idealizes, while a fashion photograph, even if specially posed or modelled or taken from an unusual angle, would inevitably have so much sheer earthiness about it that it would be more like a news item than a dream vision. Gruau, the Frenchman who created this young lady, is one of the few graphic artists who know how to capture grace and beauty of line.

Illus. 90—In America, a country whose traditions are young and thus still easily recaptured, the backward look into the past is a popular theme in advertising. The refined, slightly museum-like arrangement of the objects, placed without depth, is thoroughly graphic. The advertisement is easy to "read." This appeal in a magazine in picture-page style operates like an editorial contribution and appeals as if unintentionally, but with all the more emphasis, for the product.

Illus. 91—Double page in a men's-wear magazine from Switzerland. The ensemble is strictly informative, contenting itself with a minimum of unusual typographic features, so that its aesthetic effect is assured. The division into four pairs of rectangles is not tiring, because the pictures, though very similar in outline, have enough inner content to make them interesting. The narrow yet clear type in the first section is the only really asymmetrical element, and that is why it makes a particularly strong impression.

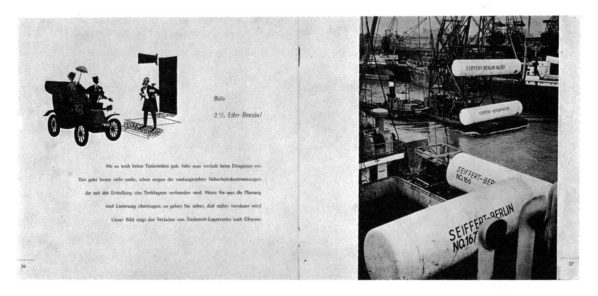

Illus. 92—Photograph and drawing complement each other. Topicality and modernity are captured in a well-planned photograph, while the graphic artist has evoked bygone days with a touch of irony. The screened type, flush on the right in this case, is so spaciously placed that an old-fashioned typeface—thoroughly justifiable here—remains easily legible and thus supports the witty theme.

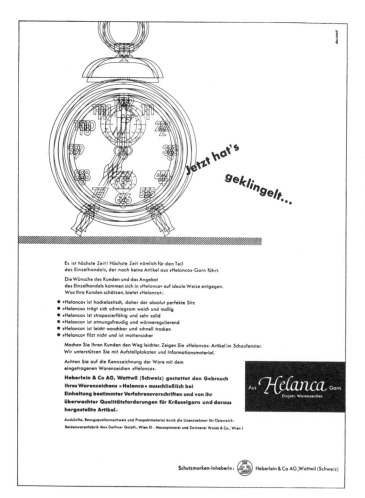

Illus. 93—The visibly clamorous alarm, the nervously reduplicated outlines of the clock and its figures, the startled exclamation—all make it abundantly clear that an hour of decision has struck. Yet the quiet flow of the groups of text, their importance brought out by the "bullets" calms the reader and simply draws his attention to the advantages of the advertised brand. The circular movement has its necessary counter-balance on the right-hand edge in the black rectangle with its distinguished lettering, conspicuously surrounded by white space. (Design by Hubert Czermak/dorland.)

Illus. 94—(Right) The ascending diagonal is the effective eye-catcher of this advertisement. From the upper block of text—at any rate from the last line, "MAYA la douce"—the eye passes easily to the theme on the right. The colorfulness of the bouquet does not subdue the more delicate floral decorations on the soap wrapper, for the white of the paper background sets it off. The shadows make a link with the second picture. The choice of flowers here is more restrained, less emotionally accentuated, for necessities are concerned —shaving requisites in this case. The rough-right lines stress the lyrical atmosphere which surrounds this advertisement like a spring breeze.

Illus. 95—Living on these carpets is heavenly—that's the idea that the unfailingly witty variations on a single theme in this series of advertisements are intended to implant in the reader's mind. The home life of the lucky owners miraculously pursues its even course as the carpets fly magically over a typical small town. An inexhaustible fund of ideas raises Lees' advertisements above the ranks of competitors. (Design by Jan Balet.)

... *those heavenly carpets by* LEES

Upstairs, downstairs,
in milady's boudoir
there's fashion in the air
when your rooms wear
Lees lovely textured carpets!
Their light and shadow surfaces
have a rich-but-casual look —
like Lees new Horizon
shown here in Ocean Green.
Visit your Lees store.
The textures will please you —
and so will the price tags!
They're the kind you'll
love to say "Yes" to.

JAMES LEES AND SONS COMPANY, BRIDGEPORT, PA., MAKERS OF LEES CARPETS AND RUGS, MINERVA AND COLUMBIA HAND-KNITTING YARNS

THE TRADE-MARK
(VERBAL AND PICTORIAL)

The name of a company is itself a perpetual advertisement. Advertising begins with the name. It is the name that makes the firm known to its customers. And when the name has succeeded in establishing itself, the firm can be recognized by it. To a certain extent, the company's name links itself to the company's goods to form a unity: it becomes identified with the quality of the product. What has been seen stays in the memory more irremovably than what has only been heard. This fact has caused a search to be made for something that would give the visual image a memorable shape: the trade-mark.

The meaning of verbal and pictorial signs must be unmistakable. The mark should leave an indelible impression at first glance, and be capable of penetrating into the unconscious so that it will rise automatically into the conscious mind when stimulated by certain ideas again.

Designing a trade-mark is a matter of teamwork, but only as far as planning and preliminary discussion are concerned, for the formal realization of the idea depends solely on artistic inspiration and on the artist's capacity

Illus. 96—The laws of harmony and contrast are equally valid for the design of trade-marks. There are two ways of making pictorial symbols. The "static" or "crystallized" form starts from a minimum requirement, usually a geometrical nucleus, which is embellished until it has gained enough distinctive features. The Mercedes sign is a classical example of a mark developed from the inside out. The Pelikan symbol obtains the same effect by the "contraction" and simplification of a natural form based on an old family coat-of-arms. Stripped of all non-essentials, it thus becomes a concentrated essence. (O. H. W. Hadank.)

Der vorsorgenden Hausfrau bietet Provins einen Weisswein an, der sich bestens eignet für den Familientisch. Angenehm, leicht, vorteilhaft, ist TROIS PLANTS ein richtiger Walliser, der weisse Alltagswein.

Fr. 1.85
die Literflasche

TROIS PLANTS

ΡRΟVΙΝS VΑLΑΙS

In gutgeführten Lebensmittelgeschäften erhältlich

Illus. 97—A newspaper advertisement by a Swiss co-operative winegrowers' association. The strong horizontals of the text are relieved by small pen and ink drawings that form a lively background to the realistically represented wine bottle. The line of stars repeats the theme of the trade-mark on the label. Intended to be valued as a symbol of quality, the trade-mark is derived from the arms of the canton of Valais.

The greatest enemy of your watch –

baffled !....

SHOCKS are the greatest enemies of a watch. Your watch is always in danger: even if you are careful, you may hit your arm against something, or your watch may slip when you are putting it on. If you visualise the minute size of the pivot of the balance-staff – this most essential and most fragile part of a watch – you will realise that but one shock is sufficient to break or twist the pivot, causing the watch to stop. Small wonder that replacing damaged balance-staffs used to be one of the watchmakers' most frequent jobs.

In the Cyma Research Department, however, an Anti-Shock Device was created which solved the problem once and for all. The Cymaflex Anti-Shock Device is a triumph of inventive genius, and its practical efficiency has proved quite extraordinary. There is no doubt that this is one of the most important and valuable inventions in the history of watchmaking. In recent years, millions of Cyma watches have been fitted with the Cymaflex Anti-Shock Device, and now a damaged Cyma balance-staff has become extremely rare. The Cymaflex Anti-Shock Device — protected by exclusive Cyma patents all over the world — is now fitted to all Cyma models. This is *one* of the reasons for the astonishing reliability of Cyma watches. See that your next watch is a Cyma!

The Cymaflex Anti-Shock Device is
protected by the following patents:

Switzerland	Germany	USA
147857	688798	2146329
198992	759135	2219068
200929	688934	2294023
208578	*France*	2219067
198197	815666	2184580
198769	854619	*England*
		528643

ONLY Cyma watches have the Cymaflex Anti-Shock-

but every **CYMA** has it !...

The Cyma Watch Co. SA of La Chaux-de-Fonds, with its works in Tavannes and Le Locle, with thousands of employees, and a world-wide Sales and Service Organization, are among the most important watchmakers in the whole world.

Illus. 98—Precision in manufacture; precision in advertising, too. The restrained, aristocratic style of this advertisement is in keeping with the company's product and also strikes the right chord in the kind of readers who are most attractive to the advertisers as potential customers. Three effective stages have been clearly worked out in this advertisement: the dynamic (and vividly colored) rectangle with the explanatory illustration, the darker circles of the photographed watches, and finally the headline, the words ONLY and CYMA and the filigree of the factory façade. (Fritz Bühler, Switzerland.)

for giving a concentrated, straightforward representation to what he has learned. The fact that the laws of harmony and contrast explained at the beginning of this book find their clearest expression precisely in this field makes it comparatively easy for the layout man and the advertising specialist to distinguish the good from the bad.

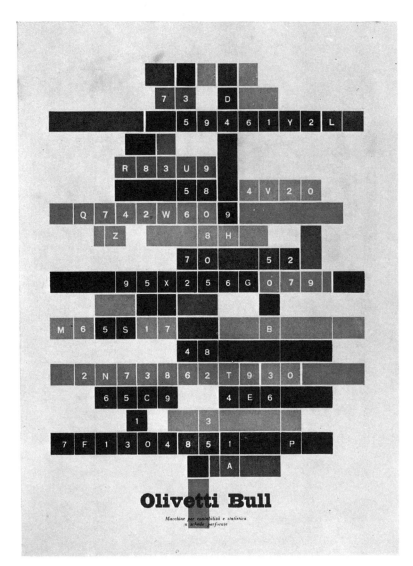

Olivetti Bull

Macchine per contabilità e statistica a schede perforate

Illus. 99—While most manu-facturers of business machines prefer naturalistic and photo-graphic advertisements, with or without living figures, Olivetti has made use almost exclusively of a graphic "telegram style" which has become an unmistakable symbol of the company. The chessboard pattern is especially effective because of its varied coloring in the verticals and horizontals.

Illus. 100—A series of six small advertisements for soft drinks. The young boy is a standard figure recurring on the delightfully colored labels and small posters. The brand name is always centrally placed; text and drawing are as coolly carefree as the consumers to whom the advertisements are addressed.

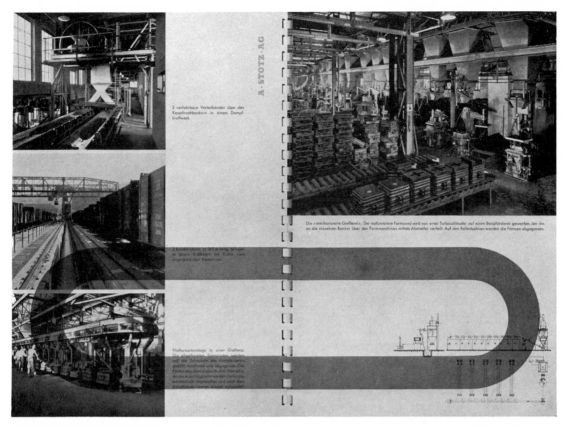

Illus. 101—Double page of a brochure for materials-handling and assembly-line equipment. Advertisements of this kind for the heavy industries are representations of a company's work: they support and supplement a specially worked-out offer. The symbol of the endlessly running belt gives life to the highly realistic photographs. The depth in space of all the photographs gives weight to an idea: the need for mechanical transport. The top picture on the left, with its foreground theme, would have been better placed below.

THE COMPANY IMAGE

It is the aim of the manufacturer of branded articles in particular to adapt and co-ordinate all his advertising, so that the prospective buyer will at once recognize all of them as belonging to the same company. The trade-mark is always the starting point, for it is the trade-mark that largely determines the appearance of the advertising in the media used. The firm's image—and it extends to the design of the factory's frontage, exhibition stands and vehicles—has color as one of its essential features. Color, like the trade-mark, can become a constant factor in advertising. Business stationery—from stickers to circular letters—has a quick-return advertising potential that is still very inadequately cultivated. It is in these small details that the task of building

an individual company image begins; if systematically expanded, it will finally cover everything the firm stands for, offers and sells.

BROCHURES, FOLDERS, CATALOGUES, HOUSE ORGANS, BUSINESS STATIONERY

The principle of double-page designing holds good here too, even if occasionally varied to conform to special conditions. Catalogues, house organs and calendars are permanent forms of advertisement. Their layouts should be distinguished and discreet rather than extravagant, static rather than lively. House organs, company magazines and almanacs intended for the trade or ultimate consumer serve to deepen the direct relationship between a business and its customers. Their external form should convey a fitting impression of the

103

Illus. 102—Layout for a client showing a double page in a brochure. The photograph has already been attached in its intended size. Caption and vignettes are drawn in. The sketched type gives the client an impression of what the advertisement will look like when it is printed. (Drawing by Peter Förster.)

seating (foam rubber)

cat. page no.	item no.	description	H	W	D	illustration	yardage	price
53	5073	Three-seater Sectional Sofa—armless	28	75	32		6 yds Satin chrome legs	273.00†
52	5074	Attached Adjustable Armrest (upholstered), specify left or right (facing)		21	6		⅓ yd Satin chrome support	16.50†
59	5080	Open-Arm Easy Chair, metal frame, wood armrests: B or TWB	27	29	29		2 yds Frame white or black enamel	135.00†
54	5087	Daybed—permanent upholstery						250.30†
54	5087-T	Daybed—grey ticking only	27	75	33		8 yds Base natural hardwood alum legs	271.40
54	5087-Z	Daybed—zipped cover on seat, permanent on back						282.90†
54	5088	Same as 5087—with bolster support						275.60†
54	5088-T	Same as 5087-T—with bolster support	27	75	33		8 yds Base natural hardwood, alum legs	296.60
54	5088-Z	Same as 5087-Z—with bolster support						308.20†
54	5089	Daybed—with permanent cover, no bolsters						162.00†
54	5089-T	Daybed—grey ticking only, no bolsters	15	75	33		5 yds Base natural hardwood alum legs	175.10
54	5089-Z	Daybed—with zipped cover, no bolsters						194.60†

†Base price only. See p. 5 for ordering instructions

HERMAN MILLER FURNITURE CO · ZEELAND, MICHIGAN

Illus. 103—Tables and statistics need a practical, easily readable structure. Nevertheless, they must have enough vitality in their arrangement and grouping of concepts to ensure that the reader will not be fatigued even after long reading. These catalogue pages make use of different plans and outlines for each group of goods. Varied typefaces and strengths of letters provide an understandable scheme of classification.

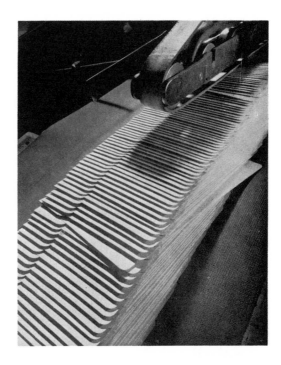

Illus. 104—Container Corporation of America, an important packaging manufacturer, has been consistently producing avant-garde advertising, designed by the foremost talents available throughout the world. It was one of the first business houses to recognize and appreciate the psychological impact of color when used on machines and tools. This double page is taken from a guide to the corporation's activities.

Illus. 105—Two primitively simple starting points are responsible for the striking impression given by this title page to a brochure. The age-old, yet always effective, color combination of red, white and black is purposefully applied. The black points in the curve of the teeth interfere with the reading-direction the eye would normally take, and thus reinforce the idea to be conveyed: the destructive effect of substances causing decay. Layouts such as this may look obvious, yet they are not always thought out so completely. (Enzo Rösli.)

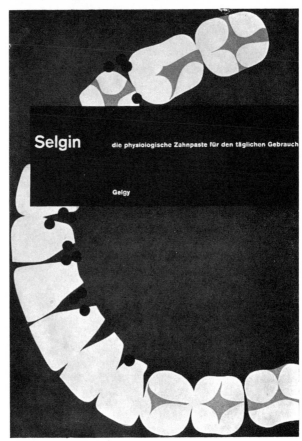

company's worth and standing. Company newspapers at a high level, apart from their advertising value, have cultural importance too, and are outstanding aids in consolidating the reputation of the company.

More than books, brochures and other printed advertising matter provide opportunities of attracting attention by the use of special kinds of paper, unusual shapes and sizes, novel methods of folding and make-up. In deciding on the dimensions to be used, a marketable starting-size of paper should be

Illus. 106—The long brand name is placed vertically on the narrow container, so that it is legible in any position. The picture of the rat explains more clearly than words the purpose of the product. Every package, unless it contains things subject to fashion or intended as gifts, should be clear, unambiguous and easily recognizable.

chosen to avoid too much waste when cutting. Attractive effects can be obtained with papers colored differently front and back, particularly when they are not folded edge to edge but have one surface overlapping. Bearing in mind the extra cost of specially made envelopes, you should envisage and plan a convenient size for the final mailing piece, ready to be placed in the envelope. Advertising literature that "swims" in its envelope is unwelcome.

Business stationery, printed matter for special occasions, and the envelope too are the house's visiting-cards. The representative style of the company should be recognizable in all its printed matter. Nothing is unimportant in this respect, not even the design of the address label for parcels.

To facilitate searching in files, it is always advisable to have the most important part of business papers on the right-hand top edge, never inside the left-hand edge. The arrangement of the text and other elements on letterheads should be repeated on other business stationery such as invoices, statements, quotations, ledger forms, and the like. For different sizes of paper, appropriate modifications can be made. It is true that the printing industry offers a great variety of free calendars and notebooks every year, but customers keep the one that has uniqueness, the unmistakably individual touch.

THE PACKAGE AND THE LABEL

Designing packages is also part of a commercial artist's work. However, working in the third dimension presents new problems. On its way from the producer to the buyer the package is placed in many different positions. Will its pulling power be equally forceful, no matter how it stands? The retailer should be presented only *one* way to stack the package in his store: with its face towards the customer so that he can see and read it. But if a package is no longer recognizable when it is placed askew, it falls short of the ideal.

Every package, like every advertisement, must be capable of retaining its pulling power even when it finds itself placed next to its most powerful rival. It must set itself apart from the rest without forfeiting the distinctive quality of its design. It should do its work just as well on the counter as in the shop window. When it is in the buyer's hand it should make him feel sure at once that he has made a good buy. Many years have passed since the days when a *good* package was the same thing as a merely beautiful one. Fitness for purpose in the materials, in the shape, size, color and text are valued more highly.

In packages, choice of color and text is determined by different factors than in other forms of advertising. The commodity is the measure: the package demands the accentuation of all emotional elements, but stresses utility at the same time. Color has a decisive part to play as it helps to guide the thoughts of the prospective buyer into the right channels. It creates associations of ideas and assists

VELISCH

Velisch KG · **Mäntel · Kostüme** · Berlin W 30 · Rankestraße 33/34 · Telefon 24 91 66

 VELISCH

Velisch KG · **Mäntel · Kostüme** · Berlin W 30 · Rankestraße 33/34 · Telefon 24 91 66

 VELISCH

Velisch KG · **Mäntel · Kostüme** · Berlin W 30 · Rankestraße 33/34 Telefon 24 91 66

VELISCH

Velisch KG
Mäntel · Kostüme
Berlin W 30 · Rankestraße 33/34
Telefon 24 91 66

Ihre Zeichen   Unser Zeichen   Berlin, den

BERLIN W 30 RANKESTRASSE 33/34 FERNRUF 24 91 66 VELISCH GESCHÄFTSLEITUNG

Postscheckkonto:
Berlin West 17 35

 VELISCH

Velisch KG
Mäntel · Kostüme
Berlin W 30 · Rankestraße 33/34
Telefon 24 91 66
Telegramme Velischmantel

GUTSCHRIFT   Datum

		DM

Bankkonten: Berliner Commersbank A.G. Berlin W 35   Postscheckkonto   Einkaufsbedingungen der deutschen Bekleidungsindustrie
Berliner Bank A.G. · Depka 41 · Berlin W 30   Berlin-West 17 35   vom 6 7 1926 einschließlich Zusatzbedingungen des DOB Verbandes
                                                                                    vom 15 1 1937 (ausgenommen Zahlungskondition)
                                                                                    Erfüllungsort für Zahlung und Lieferung Berlin-West

 VELISCH

Velisch KG · **Mäntel · Kostüme** · Berlin W 30 · Rankestraße 33/34

Illus. 107—Business stationery should be genuinely representative of the sender right down to the smallest details. Typographic form must therefore be uniform and persuasive.

identification of the package with the commodity it contains.

As for the position of the text, since two sides of the package are generally visible at the same time—or one side and one end—essential information should be located on them, one side being clearly indicated and developed as the face of the package. The design of the two major sides is frequently repeated on the third and fourth. Only one third of a can or other round package can be seen from a fixed standpoint, and only a quarter will be legible. In flat boxes, the underside is used only for unimportant information or for details which will interest the purchaser only after he has bought the goods. On the top should be only the main statements, such as the name of the company, the trade-mark, a description of the goods, and an illustration which gives the whole its distinctive note. On the second side—on upright boxes, usually the narrow side—are statements about the contents, their quality, characteristics and range of use, recipes and instructions. The co-ordination of these elements can be the task of a layout man. When preliminary drawings are being made, work should not be done flat, but in three dimensions from the start. A better survey of advertising effectiveness can thus be obtained. In every case it is advisable to ask the manufacturer of the package to supply blanks.

The importance of packaging is still growing.

Illus. 108—Packages used for brand-name products have become factors in advertising, taking the place of many a worn-out trade-mark and setting the tone for the appearance of advertising in other media. The layout of this package (shown opened out) has been consistently handled. The blocks of text on a yellow ground are well attuned to each other, and separated according to the kinds of information they have to convey. The package cannot be overlooked even in the ill-lit storeroom of the fruit grower it is intended for. (Max Schmid, Switzerland.)

Illus. 109—Art on the front pages of tourist folders has an advantage over photography: it can treat a subject in poster fashion, leaving out what is unimportant, giving the theme a more attractive background and an effective set of accessories without being less true to life than the photograph is. A colored photograph, moreover, rarely has enough vitality and emphasis to be as convincing as a good drawing. Knowledge of this fact is so widespread that all important sectors of the tourist industry make use of art, at least on the covers of their literature. Few hotels have such irreproachably photogenic façades that they will serve as good advertisements. The special atmosphere of the house can be better portrayed by graphic art. On the brochure of a hotel in the little principality of Liechtenstein, the theme and color display a positive gaiety, and the woodcut-like drawing suggests tradition and a link with the countryside.

With the exception of packs and labels for fashionable things, seasonal goods, and time-bound gift articles, there is a tendency for distinctive packages to acquire a constant visual advertising value of their own. There are many examples of successful new packs which have multiplied sales. In many cases the pack even takes over the function of a brand image which has lost its drawing power.

Every commodity should be identifiable by means of its package. The package must radiate atmosphere; it should allow the buyer when he handles it to anticipate his actual possession of the goods. Every color or composition of colors and every harmony or contrast between the various elements releases not only optical reactions, but mental ones too in the customer, encouraging or restraining his impulse to buy the goods.

TOURIST PUBLICITY

The tourist industry generally makes use of ordinary advertising media, but it occupies a unique position in the advertising world. Official and private-enterprise agencies, associations, clubs, travel bureaus, transport organi-

109

Illus. 110—No two advertisements from Paris are alike. Each year new and distinguished folders for a wide variety of prospective visitors are designed. Some of them are brightly mischievous, some composed with scrupulous scientific exactitude, but all of them have wit and charm. In this folder, Paris is depicted in photographs and keywords from A to Z. The solitary pedestrian by the "X" is the only red spot on the double page. His size and the shadow he casts make him harmonize with the content of the large photograph, and thus bring about a connection between the abstract shapes of the letters and the bustling theme of the photograph.

zations, advertise their *services*. Their aim is to encourage people interested in travel to seek a particular goal. Official or semi-official institutions stress culture, aesthetics or self-improvement, while the advertising of hotels, holiday resorts and travel agencies is characterized by the usual features of all ordinary commercial advertising, though these are never allowed to become dominant. In every case the appeal must be addressed to the feelings rather than to the intellect.

The essential advertising medium in tourism is the travel folder, which contains a wealth of possibilities as far as the arrangement of pictures and text, and variations of shape and size are concerned. The size preferred is $3\frac{7}{8} \times 8\frac{1}{4}$ inches or the double folder size $7\frac{3}{4} \times 8\frac{1}{4}$, which when folded again gives the standard folder size. Front and back pages are usually artist-designed or contain color photographs, for every folder must be capable of holding its own among a crowd of competitors who will likewise be making use of colorful, striking approaches.

The planner of travel folders has to try anew every year to arouse the interest of tourists in his region. He must either find something quite new, or use some variation on a previously discovered theme which has proved successful. Besides the basic folder, which

Illus. 111—(Below) Cover pictures drawn or built up from photographic units are customary in the United States and offer a greater wealth of possibilities in reproduction than the portrait cover for magazines which is preferred in Europe. America has a great number of magazine artists and illustrators who can satisfy the tastes of readers without imitating or vulgarizing photographs. John Atherton shows here an impression of the plains of Illinois and Iowa.

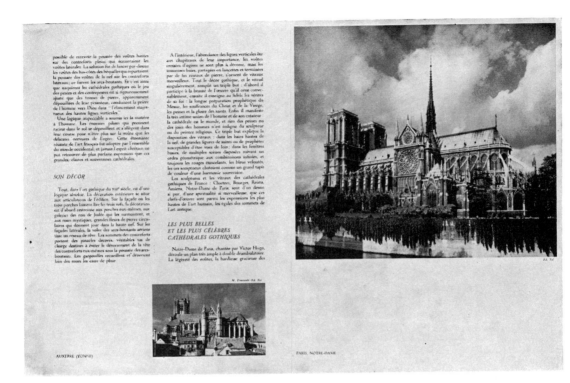

Illus. 112—Tourist folders are nearly always overloaded with illustrations; this is an outstanding exception. The calm of the architectural horizontals, seeming to lead the eye into profundity, the contrast between the verticals of the building and of the verdant walls, the central spire, which the bright cloud surrounds like a halo—all are a photographic synthesis of worldly and mystical beauty. The designer has accommodated his text and smaller picture alongside his photograph in a noteworthy arrangement of lines that does not detract from the picture.

Illus. 113—Photographs and drawings get on well with each other in tourist folders —if they serve different purposes. Drawings should never compete with photographs, but should enhance the value of the photographs by suggesting local color, by offering vignettes of people, animals, flowers, or other things typical of the landscape they are dealing with. The designer in this case sought unity in contrast and placed finely drawn sketches in two colors alongside the photographs. The layout is spacious, allowing ample room on the paper and giving free play to the fantasy of the reader.

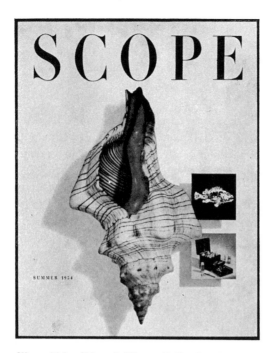

contains all the information needed by those likely to be interested, there are special folders displaying individual features of a district—events, artistic treasures, theatres, museums, local specialties and curiosities, fairs, exhibitions, gastronomic attractions.

Pictures, of course, are very important in tourist folders. No attempt should be made to show everything worth seeing, if the consequence is that each subject is reduced to postage-stamp dimensions. A small picture is only effective if it shows a subject on a large scale, seen from a wide perspective. Overcrowding with irrelevant details suppresses what is essential. Photo-montages can be used sparingly but should be recognizable as such; otherwise they will be seen and dismissed as fakes. Avoid linking-up different themes in the same picture,

such as figures in national costume and wide landscapes, by using mixtures of photographs and drawings.

Magazines and announcements of coming events are also used to draw tourists. Those issued by towns and cities to point out the charms of their local institutions and attractions are apt to suffer chiefly from a surfeit of advertisements in a wide variety of styles. This reduces the value of the editorial section, and harms the impression produced by the whole. Newspaper advertisements, sometimes printed in the form of a region's collective notices, are often unsatisfactory because they cannot be appreciated as integrated unities; seeking a co-ordinating idea in vain, the onlooker's eye is distracted by an uninteresting, motley assemblage of suspended boxes: the announcements of individual advertisers.

The most exemplary advertisers are generally government institutions and associations covering large areas promoting commerce and traffic, seaside resorts and large hotels. Switzerland, which was already carrying on systematic tourist advertising a century ago, is deservedly famous for its distinguished folders, whether they deal with the whole of Switzerland or the separate cantons, provinces, communities, hotels and transport organizations. The folders are supplemented by tourist magazines, well designed and superbly edited.

Ever since tourist advertising began, the Swiss tourist poster has held its undisputed Blue Ribbon, and has become a model for travel publicity throughout the world.

THE POSTER

The poster has always been the most magnetic of all advertising media. It is the best representative, in fact, of the essential principle of all advertising, even if it no longer stands for a definite product or idea as frequently or incisively as it once did.

Posters are rarely among the assignments of layout men. Typesetting problems on poster scale, however, are dealt with according to the same general principles as those applying to other layouts. Different concepts can be kept apart by means of white or blank colored space, to ensure a forceful effect, more easily

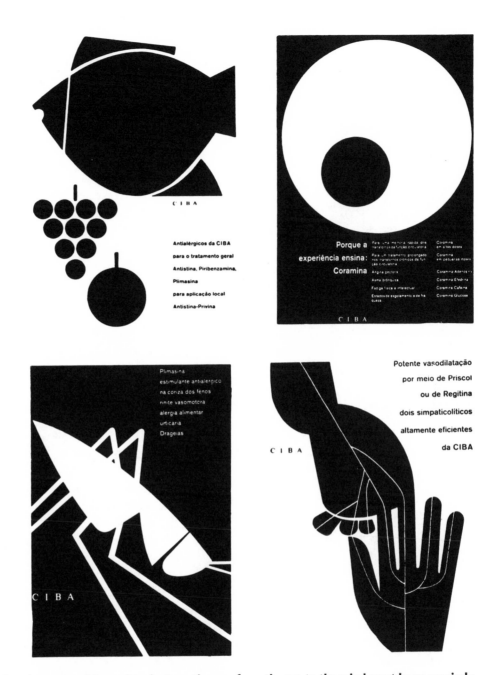

Antialérgicos da CIBA
para o tratamento geral
Antistina, Piribenzamina,
Plimasina
para aplicação local
Antistina-Privina

Porque a
experiência ensina:
Coramina

Plimasina
estimulante antialérgico
na coriza dos fenos
rinite vasomotora
alergia alimentar
urticária
Drageias

Potente vasodilatação
por meio de Priscol
ou de Regitina
dois simpaticolíticos
altamente eficientes
da CIBA

Illus. 115—In advertisements addressed to doctors, the way from the eye to the mind must be so precisely calculated that even an overworked reader will at once react as he should. The universally understandable themes are so abbreviated as to be reminiscent of traffic signs, which are likewise "unconsciously" read and at once trigger off the right impulses. The advertisements radiate security, solidity and reliability and retain their value even in the subconscious of the viewer.

than they can in ordinary advertisements. Press advertisements blown up to poster dimensions remain nothing but senselessly coarsened press advertisements: they do not have the effect of posters at all.

Reproduction and Printing Techniques

IF ALL PARTS of the layout—text, illustrations and color—have been developed successfully up to the stage of the final drawing and are ready for printing, the result can be reproduced by means of three different processes: letterpress or relief, offset lithography (a surface printing process) or by intaglio or gravure. Choice of the technique to be used in each particular case depends on the original, the task it has to fulfil, the shape and size of the sheets, the extent of the edition, and the client's requirements. But this decision should always be made before the work is started, as the character of the layout largely depends on the printing process used.

I. RELIEF PRINTING: LETTERPRESS

Printing from cast letters was invented by Gutenberg, whom we mentioned at the beginning of the book. The composition can be done by hand or by typesetting machines of various kinds. In hand-setting the text is set line by line on a composing stick and then arranged consecutively by lines on a galley. Proofs are pulled of these galleys in the hand press, to provide the proofreader, artist and possibly the client with copies for checking and dummying. After revision of the proof, the text is assembled in pages according to the layout or dummy together with the illustrations.

Setting of long text material (such as books) is done almost exclusively by means of type-setting machines, which either cast complete lines (Linotype and Intertype) or single letters (Monotype). Display type however is still largely the province of the hand-setter. While for ordinary text, layout artists manage to make do with a few machine typefaces and their variants, the artist often will choose new and unusual varieties of display typefaces to provide a wider range of expression, especially to attract attention to business and commercial advertising.

For the actual printing there are four different kinds of letterpress machines available: the hand, the platen, the cylinder and the rotary press.

Today, the hand press on which Gutenberg and his successors printed their finest work until well into the 19th century is used only for the production of proofs. However, there are societies of bibliophiles who still have their work privately printed on hand presses, and books of outstanding beauty, fine examples of

Illus. 116—In relief printing, type and pictures are raised above the non-printing surfaces. The rollers ink only the raised portions. When the paper is inserted between the press cylinder and the type-face, an impression in ink is created on the paper.

114

the printer's art at its best, are still being achieved by this means.

In the platen press, the locked-up type form is vertically positioned, inked by rollers, and pressed against the paper. All that layout artists need know about platen presses is that they are usually small in size and are primarily suitable for the printing of business stationery, package wraps, small posters, art originals in three or four colors, and advertising material on metal foil, celluloid and cellophane. The printing form can consist of rubber, linoleum or wood blocks or copper, zinc, magnesium alloy or brass etchings. The automatic cylinder presses are the most important in use for letterpress printing. Thanks to their large size and stable construction, they are particularly suitable for all kinds of good quality, difficult work, including short-run magazines and books.

The rotary presses were designed for printing on rolls of paper, which are pulled between printing cylinders on which plates have been locked. These curved plates ("stereos" made of lead or "electrotypes" made of lead or zinc with copper facing) have to be cast from the original type form. To the layout artist, this means that there will be some small loss in detail during the transfer process, although a good rotary press plate can produce results hardly distinguishable from those obtained with a cylinder press. Rotary presses run at great speed. The web is cut by a perforator either before or after it enters the machine, so that sheets are delivered to a folder attached to the end of the press. For printing large runs, for newspapers, simple advertising leaflets, circulars and supplements, rotary letterpress is unsurpassed if the requirements for the quality of the print are not too exacting.

The main problem, of course, is that illustrations must be stereotyped, and only coarse screens may be used, which almost certainly impair the quality of the illustration. To prepare art for rotary press printing, calculate on using a 65 to 85 line screen, and keep all details strong.

Platen and cylinder presses can also be used to die-cut unusual patterns for packages. Sharp-edged strip steel is inserted in wooden beds and used instead of the printing form.

REPRODUCTION OF ILLUSTRATIONS

Nowadays woodcuts, linoleum cuts, and other relief-process blocks made by hand are reserved almost exclusively for artistic work. This type of illustration can serve occasionally also for ceremonial publications, testimonials, diplomas and tipped-in book illustrations. There is no need to use original blocks however, as metal engravings can be produced mechanically from drawn originals; the photographing is much easier than hand cutting and the results are indistinguishable.

The photo-engraver makes line blocks or zinc etchings (etchings in relief without halftones) from any line originals, showing only sharply defined points, lines and surfaces. A photographic negative is made in the desired size from the black-and-white drawing. This negative (on glass or film) is copied on to a prepared light-sensitive zinc or copper plate and etched so that nothing is left on the metal but the lines of the actual drawing. Errors can be corrected by hand, by being cut away or chiselled out. Finally, the line block is attached ("mounted") type-high to a wooden or lead base.

All monochrome or black-and-white drawings are suitable for line blocks—pen and brush drawings made with India ink, mezzotint engravings, music, handwriting, monochrome lithographs, prints of woodcuts and linoleum cuts, maps or ordinary type copy. Line blocks for printing in several colors can be prepared from a multi-colored drawing by an artist; he traces the original drawing as many times as there are colors, but in black and white, on acetate overlays—one for each color. Varicolor effects can be achieved by overlapping (surprinting)—green from blue and yellow, for example.

Line drawings are usually made two or three times larger than the final plate, so that the lines will appear prominently and clearly in the reproduction. In making enlargements from an original, the lines generally become ragged and unclear. But, if the size is very much reduced (to less than 25% of the original), the drawing often turns out to be unattractively compressed and an undesirable impression is obtained. In such cases, moreover, interim photographs are then necessary and these increase the cost.

Dies or etchings of brass or other hard metal from line originals are needed by the bookbinder for stamping covers. These are like line etchings but have steep edges so that they will stand out clearly from the base. Drawings for stamping must be bold and clear.

Halftone etching is a modern art that has increased the range of all printed illustrations. Halftones of course only convey the impression of tone—for in enlargements they stand revealed as black and white dots of varying size and intensity. The whole picture produced by a halftone is a network in which the "half" tones make up a chessboard pattern with black and white alternating in equal parts. But there are also quartertones (one-quarter black and three-quarters white) and three-quarter tones naturally having reversed values, as well as other values from, say 10% to 90%. In a halftone, a pure black surface or one unbroken by points is just as impossible to obtain as a pure white without points. This is because of the process by which a halftone is made.

The picture is divided up by means of a screen placed close to a light-sensitive plate or film. Actually the screen consists of two glass plates cemented together. On each glass, fine parallel lines have been engraved in such a way that the lines on each glass are at right angles to each other and form a network. Screens vary from 40 to 200 lines per inch. The light rays reflected from the object (the photograph to be engraved, for example) have to pass through the small openings on the screen between the lens and the photographic plate before they touch the plate. The photograph is thus broken up into small dots by the screen.

A negative (the reverse of the photographic print) is then transferred to a metal (usually copper or an alloy) plate, just as line etchings are made. In fact, the dot-broken negative is now a line (dot) film as there are no longer any continuous tones in it.

While the halftone process is fascinating, the layout artist need be concerned only with preparing proper copy. Since strong blacks and whites will be broken into dots, photographic originals must be retouched. They may then look artificial to the naked eye, but will reproduce to good advantage. If reproduction photographs show defects these will be more noticeable in the final halftone. Photographs of machinery, for instance, always look unattractive unless they are touched up. A good retouch artist knows how to make greys and to avoid very delicate tones in a photograph, as well as a hundred other tricks of the trade. He can make your layout sparkle or look dull.

Polychrome (multi-color) originals are engraved into "process color" halftones by mechanical means too complicated for the layout man. Suffice to say that for every full-color picture, whether a photograph or a drawing, at least four separate printing plates are needed to obtain most of the colors found in nature. In process work, engravers and printers rely on the fact that yellow and blue make green, blue and red make violet, red and yellow make orange, and black is a mixture of all three primary colors. To get depth, richness of tone and adequate detail, a separate black plate is essential. The colored inks are superimposed on each other in the press.

All gaily colored subjects and motifs are suitable as originals for process color engravings, no matter whether they are drawn, painted, photographed in color, or colored as contact prints, enlargements or transparencies.

Many layouts containing both black and white and halftones (for example, photographs with inserted text) can be made into a single plate—a combination line and halftone etching. Copy must be prepared specially if the result is to be neat. Attach to the basic copy the part of the design intended for the halftone. Provide it with a covering sheet and register marks (tiny cross lines). On the basic copy, place the text and everything else that is to be line-etched if in "same size," with cross lines where the halftone goes, so all will "register" properly. In other words, the register marks will tell the engraver where the inserted halftone negative is to be correctly placed in relation to the rest of the copy. The engraver will make his screened halftone negative, and then the line negative, including any text (or two line negatives if the line drawing needs reduction). Then he will strip the two negatives together on glass and

Illus. 117—A photograph as seen through four halftone screens of varying densities. The finer the screen, the more justice is done to the delicate gradations of the original. Coarse-screened photo-engravings can only reproduce with rough gradations. The retoucher works on the photograph and thus compensates for the disadvantages that will be caused by the dissolution of the picture into screens and dots.

(Left above). A No. 65 screen for newspaper printing on coarse cellulose-pulp paper.

(Right above). A No. 75 screen for printing on machine-glazed paper.

(Left below). A No. 100 screen for calender-finished or other well glazed paper.

(Right below). A No. 133 screen, suitable for satin-finished and art coated papers.

Illus. 118—Comparative dissolutions of a picture by letterpress and photogravure (intaglio) screens. The letterpress screen is inserted, for the reproduction of a picture, between the lens and the negative so that it breaks the picture up into dots or squares. A chessboard pattern is formed where black and white are equally intense in halftones. In the gravure screen the light-colored lines remain after etching, while the more-or-less dark squares form cavities etched at varying depths according to their strength.

117

transfer the images to a metal plate. Finally the combined work is etched. The well-graduated tones of the drawing or photograph will then show the characteristic breaking-up into dots, while the line portion will appear without dots.

STEREOTYPE AND ELECTROTYPE

Type and original halftone plates show signs of wear after they have been used for large runs. If more than 20,000 impressions are to be printed, stereos are usually made of text, line etchings and coarse-screened halftones, while electrotypes are made of fine halftones. (As we have seen, curved stereos are used for printing on a rotary press.)

It is important for a designer to realize that another step away from the original art is thus necessary. A matrix will be made from the printing form. This is composed either of papier-mâché, pressed when moist on to the printing and picture form (for a stereo), or of wax poured on as a liquid and allowed to dry into a matrix or mould (for an electro). Each matrix reproduces the printing form negatively. Next step for a stereo is a casting in metal—either flat, or curved—made from this "mat." This gives a more or less exact image of the original type and simple picture forms. For an electrotype, after the impression has been made, the wax is dusted with graphite and suspended on a copper rod in an electrolytic bath. The copper deposit forms a thin layer which is then cast on to type metal and made type-high for relief printing.

2. SURFACE PRINTING: LITHOGRAPHY

Lithography, both direct and "offset," is based in principle on a physical fact: that grease repels water. In direct lithography, impressions are made from a certain kind of stone directly on to the paper. In offset printing, a rubber blanket receives an ink impression from the printing plate and transfers it to the paper, so that the printing plate never touches the paper.

Direct lithography is seldom used in modern work as it requires an artist who can draw with a greasy ink, pencil or chalk on the litho stone, a calcareous slate. This stone has a fine-grained surface which breaks the artwork

into small dots, much like a halftone, and delicate shadings can be reproduced. When the stone is etched, the greasy areas repel the acid; they retain the impression when the stone is inked and put through a press. The process is fine for artists who want to create drawings and produce a dozen to a hundred copies, and is especially good for big posters in bright colors, but the work is limited by the size of the stone and the fact that large editions wear off the impression.

This disadvantage can be somewhat overcome by having the artist make his drawing on the small stone, pull a proof or two, then have him erase his work (this can be done) except for his guide lines, and replace it with a second drawing or a second color, and so on, until a number of works or a multi-color work is produced and proofed in separate black-and-white proofs. Now the proofs can be photographed and made into zinc line etchings (not halftones) or offset films. These are then assembled for color printing, or the many different drawings are assembled for printing on a large press, and run off in any quantity. Surely this suggests numerous opportunities for unusual effects to the creative designer.

Photo-lithography long ago took over from direct art litho. The photographic negatives for planography (surface printing) are like those for letterpress printing; they are transferred to the stone, which has been made light-sensitive, and then further etched. Only the light-struck areas remain with the impression.

In offset lithography, the interposing of a rubber blanket between plate and paper makes

Illus. 119—In direct lithography the copy to be reproduced is reversed on the stone and, after inking, is directly printed on to the paper which is inserted between the press and the stone.

all the difference. A thin, flexible zinc (alloy) offset printing plate is photographically made from stripped-up negatives, attached around a cylinder, and locked into place. Moistening and inking rollers alternately pass over it, or rather the plate on the cylinder revolves across the rollers. In one segment of its rotation, the plate picks up ink which it transfers on the next part of its trip to the rubber blanket covering another cylinder. This rubber cylinder on half of its revolution picks up the impression and applies it on the other half of its trip to the paper. The elasticity of the rubber sheet ensures that the ink is impressed almost faultlessly even on paper with a rough surface. The surface of offset paper is specially "sized" (see Paper) for litho.

Offset is the best method for printing illustrated work on sheets of large size in black or in many colors rapidly and inexpensively. A certain softness of contours in the outlines can be a minor drawback or an asset. The layout man given a choice of printing process for a job should always consider the advantages this process offers.

With constant innovations in copying and printing techniques, with machines of improved designs, with bimetal and trimetal plates that allow printing on coated papers, with printing also possible on papers with granular or uneven surfaces (as well as cloth, plastic and acetate), offset is continually attracting new clients.

The designer may prefer the sharpness of letterpress, but offset will often be chosen nevertheless, because of its greater economy. Offset and gravure—processes which until quite recently were still in their infancy—have made great conquests at the expense of letterpress printing. Photo-composition on film and other quite recent advances in methods of typesetting help offset more than letterpress, and innovations in color separation of polychrome illustrations apply equally to lithography. Designers will find that clients primarily attracted by low costs come back again and again to offset because it is more adaptable as well.

Small offset printing machines (such as multiliths) have succeeded in taking their place among the duplicating machines in offices for printing short runs in throw-away advertising literature. These machines follow the general principles of offset printing, but use thin metal foils or "plates." These can be marked by hand with a special India ink or chalk, or supplied with text direct from the ordinary typewriter. Typeset and photographs are transferred photographically. The advantages are that medium-size runs (5,000 or so) of small page size circulars are inexpensive, need not be unattractive, and proofreading and setting-up need little time. Also the plates are easily interchangeable and can easily be stored.

3. PHOTOGELATIN PRINTING

Widely used for cheap picture postcards, photogelatin printing also can produce wonderfully beautiful colored reproductions of paintings. The process uses glass plates on cylinder presses. A light-sensitive layer of gelatin is applied to the surface of a glass plate where, placed in a drying chamber, it acquires a finely corrugated, granular surface. A negative made photographically from the original is retouched and exposed on to the plate. In the development of the glass plate, the exposed portions of the picture are rendered more or less insoluble according to the quantity of light they have received. The unexposed parts retain moisture during printing which repels the ink. The plate thus accepts ink corresponding to the tones of the original, and this shaded image is transferred in printing to the paper. Photogelatin is a process for small editions, as the glass plates do not stand up to long and heavy use.

4. GRAVURE: INTAGLIO PRINTING

There are various types of gravure—both sheet-fed and rotary-fed—with copper or steel plates engraved and etched, or produced by broken-dot screens—but in all methods the upper surface of a gravure plate is un-inked and non-printing, and the image is incised below the surface (intaglio).

In copperplate or steel engraving, the drawing is engraved by means of a tool—a "graver." Ink is rubbed into the cuts by hand or machine. The surface is then cleaned,

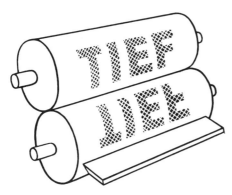

Illus. 120—In gravure, pictures and lettering are engraved through a screen into squares and etched at various depths into a copper cylinder. This cylinder rotates in a thin ink and the excess is wiped off by the doctor blade before the paper comes into contact with the cylinder. The paper draws its impressions out of the cavities which have been filled with ink. See Illus. 118.

usually with a cloth. In printing, the paper takes the ink from the incisions in the metal.

Etchings, on the other hand, are not engraved but etched in. The etcher uses a needle to expose parts of the metal surface of a plate that have been covered with an acid-proof coating. The processed plate is then etched and used for printing in the same way as the copperplate. There are many kinds of engraving and etching, for both of these processes have been much used by artists for centuries. Dürer and Rembrandt engraved or etched many of their best known works.

Just as with woodcuts and other hand techniques, multi-colored etchings are possible, but in most cases color weakens the distinctive characteristics of the etching.

The type of intaglio printing uniquely important for commerce generally is called gravure, sometimes photogravure or roto-gravure, because the process uses photographic engraving and the press plate rotates. Text and illustrations are not assembled until final montage. Generally, however, and particularly in the case of Sunday newspaper supplements, magazines, advertising leaflets and the like, the typesetter and gravure photographer each need copies of the layout. The typesetter pulls proofs of his "hot" metal type in black on cellophane. The photographer makes a continuous tone negative in layout size from the illustration and from this prepares a contact (positive) transparency correctly reproducing all the tones of the original.

The transparencies of the text and illustrations are then assembled on the montage table, all films being attached to a glass plate lying on a firm sheet illuminated from below.

The gravure screen which is interposed between the glass plate and the printing plate is used to screen its whole montage—type and all—causing a grain to appear in the type. The screen differs from the halftone screen in that white lines are used to divide the picture into uniform squares. The depth of the squares varies according to the amount of light acting on them. The cavities enclosed by the engraved squares in the plate, when put on press, will accept varying quantities of ink to transfer to paper.

The printing, whether on a roll-fed or sheet-fed press, is the same. The etched copper plate is wrapped around a press cylinder, which is briefly immersed as it revolves in a tank containing thinly flowing gravure ink. Before the ink comes into contact with the paper, which runs over another cylinder, a long and sharp steel blade called a "doctor" removes all the ink outside the cavities. The white cross-hatched pattern of the screen will perhaps still be recognizable in the most brightly lighted places. However, the absorbent paper used for gravure makes the depths merge into each other and produce velvety shading, the quality that makes gravure ideal for the reproduction of richly toned and colored pictures.

Copperplate rotogravure plates can be used for long-run illustrated editions that need to be printed in a short time, on the cheapest kind of paper, at low cost.

As the copper cylinder may be damaged by sand, dust or a doctor blade that is not quite smooth, it is often chromium-plated.

5. SILK-SCREEN PROCESS PRINTING

Fabric-screen process printing is not, strictly speaking, a printing process at all as it does not require a press: drawn originals are reproduced on paper, glass, plastic foils, fabrics, wood, etc., when ink is forced with a squeegee through a fine sieve of textile on to the material to be printed.

A narrow-meshed screen of the silk or other fabric is stretched on a frame of wood or light metal. It is secured to a base plate by means of a hinge so that it always keeps the same position when the paper is positioned for printing. The sieve is made partly impervious to ink by means of covering foils or paint, or by photographic means. The ink, introduced on to the screen along one of the sides of the frame, is spread evenly by a squeegee of wood or rubber across the screen to the other edge of the frame. As it moves, the squeegee forces ink through the open meshes on to the paper. After a run, the screen can be washed out or loosened from the stencil and made ready for the next color. As the inks used are usually opaque, care must be taken in multi-color work to see that the correct color sequence is followed.

Silk-screen, formerly used only for printing on fabrics, is now being increasingly employed for advertising work. Electrically powered machines for printing by this process are now available. Chiefly used for printing posters, show cards and package wraps from colored originals, silk-screened business stationery is unusual looking as the three-dimensional application of color gives something of the appearance of a steel engraving. Like all other methods of printing, silk-screen printing may be used in combination with letterpress printing.

The layout man will find artists who can cut screens and photo-engravers who can make screens more plentiful than stone litho artists.

6. PAPER

Paper has been manufactured from many raw materials—rags, wood pulp, chemically decomposed wood, cellulose, straw, esparto, to name some. The great strength of rag fibres makes them a valuable basic material, but as the supply of rags is inadequate, they are used only when highly durable papers are needed for securities, technical drawing paper, official documents, bank notes and the like.

"Groundwood" or "mechanical" pulp is produced from wood which is pulverized by rotating grindstones. Pulping by this process fails to dissolve certain ingredients in the wood, and the result is decomposition and yellowing of the paper. Therefore groundwood papers (newsprint) are only used for less valuable printing work, such as newspapers and paper-back books.

"Chemical pulp" — from chemically disintegrated wood — provides longer fibres of cellulose, which are purer, finer and more flexible than mechanical pulp, and therefore less fragile and more permanent in color.

Up to 30% of filler—fine earth, china clay, titanium or plaster—is added to all paper pulp to make it fuller and denser. An addition of "size" (glue or resin) to fill in the pores enables the paper to take ink. Blotting and filter papers are made without any addition of size, so that they will remain absorbent.

Papers are divided into three classes according to their structure (omitting the small number of special papers):

Rag papers contain neither mechanical nor chemical pulp, if sold as 100% rag. High quality stationery may contain only 25% rag.

So-called "wood-free" papers contain no mechanical pulp fibres—all chemical pulp. "Wood-free" is of course an inaccurate term, but is used since cellulose from chemical wood pulp has quite different properties from its starting product.

Medium-fine paper contains, in addition to chemical pulp fibres, up to 75% mechanical pulp fibres. Its strength decreases according to the amount of mechanical pulp fibres it contains.

A distinction is made between writing papers, drawing papers, printing papers, packaging papers, and special papers.

Printing papers are again subdivided according to the printing process for which they are intended, such as offset.

Machine-finished paper may receive no further treatment after it has passed through the paper-making machine. Papers have two sides—a wire or rough side and a felt or fuzzier side. The better the grade of paper the more alike the two sides are. To overcome "two-sidedness," paper is often finished in certain ways. For example, to obtain a somewhat glazed, closed surface without coating,

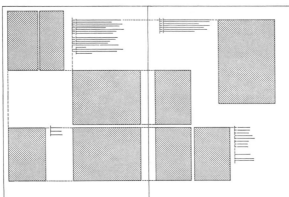

Illus. 121—A double page of "Graphis Annual," a publication which not only reproduces every year the top achievements of graphic and advertising art, but is itself a model of first-class layout. The schematic drawing makes it clear that the picture-groups on the left with the text are admirably attuned to each other, while the eye-catching point above on the right offers a novelty to contrast with the whole.

but with a "satin" finish, the paper can be "calendered" by being put through a series of smooth rollers. This makes the two surfaces more alike and more suitable for halftone printing.

Coated (art) papers have a fine layer of casein brushed on. This surface permits fine-screened printing, as it is almost perfectly compact and smooth. Special coated papers are made for offset work.

Papers are sometimes plated with metal foils for use in the packaging industry. There are also laminated and wood-plated papers for wallpapers, interior decoration and furniture manufacture.

The direction of the paper "grain" is of great importance in the printing of books and wrappers, as paper printed cross-grain is apt to "creep" under the influence of moisture, causing unattractive changes of shape to occur. The grain is easy to note—simply fold a sheet and see which direction gives you the clearer fold line. The grain should correspond to the running direction—the way in which the paper passes through the paper-making machine. Books must be printed so that the grain is parallel with the book's spine, as the moisture in the bookbinding adhesive causes expansion which gives the folded sheets a wavy form if bound cross-grain. In offset printing, especially on color work, the grain of the paper must be parallel to the axis of the printing cylinder since a correctly laid paper in its inevitable expansion clings closely to the cylinder—otherwise pleats may occur.

The weight of paper is also important in all printing. Consult with your printer and paper house as antiquated methods of computing paper weights are still used. Check paper weight carefully—printed matter to be sent by mail requires that certain weight limits must not be exceeded, or extra postage will be assessed.

The thickness of paper in relation to its height is called its bulk. If a publisher wishes to make a book with a small number of pages look like a much larger work, he uses thick, loose, bulky paper.

For advertising purposes, choice of the right kind, color and brightness of paper is very important. Every paper, even one that is apparently pure white, has a character of its own. A faint yellowish tone is pleasanter than a bluish one, which tends to look cold and impersonal. Colored papers must be dyed in pulp to give them a faultless composition, as mechanical pulp causes varying reactions on inks and affects appearance.

Letterpress printing with halftones can only be done on coated paper or on paper with a glossy surface, but over the long run it is pleasanter to read print on "mat" (wove, vellum, or offset) paper than on paper which so strongly reflects light. Choose your paper in relation to the printing process which will reproduce your art work best.

Transparency of the paper may be another disturbing factor, particularly if the paper is to be printed on both sides. If it is, preference should be given to less transparent papers with a relatively small wood content.

A LAST WORD

Subjects not immediately concerned with layout work have been omitted or dealt with briefly so that this book would not be overburdened. For all those interested, there are good books available in every technical, manufacturing, advertising and artistic sector involved. The steady progress going on in all departments of advertising is particularly reflected in the magazines which deal with both topical happenings and important future prospects. Some magazines outside the scope of the professional sphere are noteworthy for their fine composition and their exemplary layout in the editorial sections, as the value of good design is being increasingly recognized by publishers and editors.

Important, too, for a rewarding survey of creative work over a longer period of time are the artists' yearbooks, which throughout are similarly notable for their good layout. The study of this material is stimulating, and it encourages unusual, attractive and effective work.

INDEX